# On

# Righteousness, Oaths, and Usury

## A Commentary on Psalm 15

# Sources in Early Modern Economics, Ethics, and Law

## General Editors

**Jordan J. Ballor**, Acton Institute
**Stephen J. Grabill**, Acton Institute

The disciplines of economics, ethics, and law cannot be detached from a historical background that was; it is increasingly recognized, religious in nature. Economists Adam Smith and Léon Walras drew on the work of sixteenth- and seventeenth-century Spanish theologians who strove to understand the process of exchange and trade in order to better articulate subjective value, a dynamic theory of money, the role of the merchant, and the concept of marginal utility. Likewise, political theorists John Neville Figgis and Otto von Gierke drew on the work of sixteenth- and seventeenth-century Dutch, Swiss, German, and Spanish jurists and ethicists who articulated concepts that laid the foundation for federalist political structures, constitutionalism, popular sovereignty, natural-law jurisprudence, and limited government in the Western legal tradition. After a long period in which economics, ethics, and law became detached from theology, many economists, legal scholars, political theorists, and theologians now see the benefit of studying early modern economic, ethical, and legal texts in their full cultural, often religious, context. This series, *Sources in Early Modern Economics, Ethics, and Law*, provides first-ever English translations and editions of some of the most formative but previously inaccessible texts that shaped the disciplines of economics, ethics, and law in the early modern era and beyond. These inexpensive translations of seminal texts will make substantive contributions to contemporary interdisciplinary discussion.

## Editorial Board

# On Righteousness, Oaths, and Usury

## A Commentary on Psalm 15

Wolfgang Musculus

Translated by Todd M. Rester

Introduction by Jordan J. Ballor

CLP Academic

Grand Rapids · Michigan

Refo500

*On Righteousness, Oaths, and Usury: A Commentary on Psalm 15*



Translated by Todd M. Rester

Cover image: Fuggerei nachts
License: Creative Commons Attribution 3.0 Unported
Photo credit: Wolfgang B. Kleiner
URL: http://commons.wikimedia.org/wiki/File:Fuggerei_nachts.jpg
Inset photo: Wikimedia Commons (http://commons.wikimedia.org/wiki/File:Wolfgang-Musculus.jpg)



ISBN: 978-1-938948-72-5

CHRISTIAN'S LIBRARY PRESS
*An imprint of the Acton Institute for the Study of Religion & Liberty*
98 E. Fulton
Grand Rapids, Michigan 49503
Phone: 616.454.3080
Fax: 616.454.9454
www.clpress.com

*Interior composition by Judy Schafer*
*Proofreading by Geoffrey Grissom*
*Cover design by Peter Ho*
*Editorial assistance by Andrew M. McGinnis*

Printed in the United States of America

# Contents

## Sources in Early Modern Economics, Ethics, and Law

# Series Introduction

*Jordan J. Ballor*
*Stephen J. Grabill*

For the same underlying reasons that moral theology is held in disrepute by many Western intellectuals, modern economists tend to glibly dismiss or even simply ignore the economic ideas of the scholastics, whether those of the twelfth or the seventeenth century. For many intellectuals nowadays, moral theology has come to signify a passé form of religious thinking that embraces irrationality and dogmatism, and economic historians—along with notable astrophysicists, geneticists, paleontologists, political analysts, philosophers, and ethicists—have all espoused this line of thought. Among the latter, in particular, the identification of scholastic economics (or the "canonical concept of market behavior," as it is sometimes called) with Aristotelian metaphysics and ecclesiastical authority has made modern economic professionals reticent or, at the very least unreceptive, to acknowledging any sophisticated analytical contribution to monetary and value theory by the Schoolmen or the Doctors—their sixteenth- and seventeenth-century heirs.

The severing of economic ideas from their original historical and metaphysical contexts becomes especially pronounced in the contemporary debate over the prehistory of economics. Invariably, most mainstream economic historians locate the birth of modern economics in Adam Smith, the mercantilists, and the physiocrats. For historian of economics Mark Blaug, the prehistory of economics begins with the seventeenth-century mercantilists and not, as the revisionists insist, with either the ancient Greeks or the medieval scholastics. He coins the term *pre-Adamite economics* to methodologically define and restrict the era of prehistory to Smith's immediate and direct historical precursors: the seventeenth-century mercantilists, the physiocrats, and the British free-trade writers of the eighteenth century.

The broader question of whether the prehistory of economics should start in the thirteenth century or much earlier is, in Blaug's estimation, "an afterthought."[1] An afterthought, we might infer, which could presumably surface information that would challenge positivist assumptions about human behavior and social cohesion and one that will yield few, if any, new insights into quantitative methods and models. Where the scholastics analyzed economic and commercial transactions as either ethical or legal matters involving the application of natural law to civil contracts, "it was the mercantilists," contends Blaug, "who, long before Adam Smith, broke with the canonical conception of market behavior as a moral problem and fashioned the concept of 'economic man.'" These mercantilists

> believed in the direct power of self-interest and in matters of domestic economic policy came near to advocating laissez-faire. Adam Smith was not the first to have confidence in the workings of the 'invisible hand.' Nor is it necessary to

1. Mark Blaug, *Economic Theory in Retrospect*, 5th ed. (Cambridge: Cambridge University Press, 1997), 29.

> appeal to scholastic influences to account for his grasp of the determination of prices by demand and supply.[2]

Regardless of whether it is necessary to appeal to scholastic influences to explain how Smith, in particular, understood price and value to be determined, such a determination does not speak to the wider issue of whether such seminal figures in the history of economics as Bernardo Davanzati (1529–1606), Hugo Grotius (1583–1645), Samuel von Pufendorf (1632–1694), Gershom Carmichael (1672–1729), Francis Hutcheson (1694–1746), Jean-Jacques Burlamaqui (1694–1748), Adam Ferguson (1723–1816), Ferdinando Galiani (1728–1787), Auguste Walras (1801–1866), and Léon Walras (1834–1910) were influenced by scholastic treatments of price and value. Neither does this judgment determine, for that matter, whether Smith's entire system of thought remains intelligible if the role he assigns to teleology, final causes, divine design, and virtue is disregarded as merely ornamental.[3] In this wider respect, therefore, the modern quibble over scholastic influences in Smith is a red herring because, as Langholm attests, it sidesteps serious historical investigation into the continuities and discontinuities between scholastic and modern economic ideas.[4] Furthermore, it also has the convenient side effect of

---

2. Blaug, *Economic Theory in Retrospect*, 31.

3. See James E. Alvey, "The Secret, Natural Theological Foundation of Adam Smith's Work," *Journal of Markets & Morality* 7, no. 2 (Fall 2004): 335–61. See also Paul Oslington, ed., *Adam Smith as Theologian* (New York: Routledge, 2011).

4. "From an analytical and terminological point of view," writes Langholm, "there is much of scholastic teaching that can be seen to have survived into modern economics. This is not surprising, since (at least if this observation is limited to our Western civilization) it was in the high Middle Ages that the foundations were laid for the kind of systematic reasoning about social relationships that has run on continually to the present day. Sometimes, as in the case of the fairness of the market price, it was deemed pertinent above to point out a subtle shift in the moral basis that supported an apparently unaltered doctrine. Elsewhere, where doctrines

downplaying the importance of teleology and natural theology in the thought of Smith himself and other seventeenth-, eighteenth-, and nineteenth-century political economists.

By methodologically constricting the prehistory of economics to the mercantilists and the physiocrats, as positivist historiographers commend, economic history congeals around such characteristically "modern" concerns as the concept of "economic man," self-interest, and the emancipation of economics from the so-called canonical concept of market behavior. This arbitrary limitation of which ideas and which people carry weight in economic history only serves to bolster twentieth-century positivist assumptions, particularly those of value neutrality and *homo economicus*, the assumption that humans act as rational and self-interested agents who desire wealth, avoid unnecessary labor, and seek to order their decision making exclusively around those goals. In the end, the modern reduction of the prehistory of economics to the seventeenth-century mercantilists can be put in the form of an Occam's razor-like question: Why appeal to scholastic influences to illumine modern notions of money,

---

have changed as radically as in the case of lending at interest, the scholastics can still be credited with posing the terms of an ongoing argument. Therefore, it would seem that much of the old vessel remained to receive new content. The question is how completely it was ever emptied of the ferment prepared for it in the medieval schools. This subject requires a book rather than a few lines. In fact, it has been the subject of many books, some of them provoked or inspired by Max Weber's ideas about religion and capitalism. For simplicity, let us recall that scholastic economics rested on three intellectual traditions. The first support was the tradition of the Bible and the Church Fathers with its emphasis on individual duty. The second was the tradition of the recently rediscovered Roman law with its emphasis on individual rights. The two traditions were made to balance briefly and precariously in the Thomist synthesis by means of a third support in Aristotelian social philosophy." See Odd Langholm, "Scholastic Economics," in *Pre-Classical Economic Thought: From the Greeks to the Scottish Enlightenment*, ed. S. Todd Lowry (Boston/Dordrecht/Lancaster: Kluwer Academic Publishers, 1987), 132–33.

value, and price when all the basic elements of classical economics are already embedded in mercantilism?

The most straightforward reply is that seminal ideas, which include revolutionary economic ideas, never develop in intellectual, historical, religious, philosophical, or geographical vacuums. "Enlightened," secular reaction to the medieval Church's temporal jurisdiction and to theology's intellectual hegemony as the queen of the sciences has created a modern milieu in which scholars are no longer even aware of the historical influence that fundamental Christian doctrines have exerted in Western culture and university life.[5] From very early times, Christian theologians assumed that the application of patterns of discursive reasoning (as in the scholastic method, which was a method instituted by medieval Christian theologians and adapted and applied for subsequent centuries) could yield an increasingly accurate understanding not only of God's word and moral will but also of the created order itself.

Thus the systematic application of reason to a variety of intellectual undertakings, including economic problems, was not the invention of the Enlightenment. Rather, the application of reason within a coherent intellectual framework is the legacy of Christian scholasticism—the method of the medieval and early modern schools. The application of this scholastic method led to increased understanding of the world and human affairs, and spurred efforts to formulate logical explanations of regular occurrences in nature. "All things possess order amongst themselves: this order is the form that makes the world resemble God," wrote Dante in the *Divine Comedy*.[6] It can be argued that the specific application of scholastic method to economic

5. See Chris L. Firestone and Nathan Jacobs, eds., *The Persistence of the Sacred in Modern Thought* (Notre Dame: University of Notre Dame Press, 2012).

6. Dante, *Paradise*, trans. Anthony Esolen (New York: Modern Library, 2004), 1:103–5, p. 9.

problems became the seedbed for innovative ideas that, after much dialectical refinement, came to shape the world of modern economics. The truth of this statement does not rest on modernity's own understanding of its birth, development, or future trajectory but rather on the demonstrable "internal interconnections and affinities among ideas, their dynamism or 'particular go' (Lovejoy's phrase), and the logical pressures they are capable of exerting on the minds of those that think them."[7]

Assent to this claim, however, will require the positivist historian to reconsider not only the relationship between metaphysical schemata and intellectual traditions, which, in turn, will require an acknowledgement of the indispensable role of theological doctrines in the history of ideas,[8] but it will also require an admission that the recent detachment of economics from morality is itself a novelty, an aberration from a long-standing tradition within political economy itself.[9] In Alvey's judgment,

---

7. Francis Oakley, *Natural Law, Laws of Nature, Natural Rights: Continuity and Discontinuity in the History of Ideas* (New York and London: Continuum, 2005), 9.

8. See Oakley, *Natural Law, Laws of Nature, Natural Rights*, 13–34. See also the various essays in Oakley's *Politics and Eternity: Studies in the History of Medieval and Early-Modern Political Thought* (Leiden: Brill, 1999); Oakley, *Omnipotence, Covenant, and Order: An Excursion in the History of Ideas from Abelard to Leibniz* (Ithaca: Cornell University Press, 1984); Oakley, *Kingship: The Politics of Enchantment* (Oxford: Blackwell Publishing, 2006); and William J. Courtenay, *Covenant and Causality in Medieval Thought: Studies in Philosophy, Theology, and Economic Practice* (London: Variorum Reprints, 1984).

9. Broadly, on the historical constriction and positivism of contemporary economic thinking, see John D. Mueller, *Redeeming Economics: Rediscovering the Missing Element* (Wilmington, DE: ISI Books, 2010). See also Jeffrey T. Young, *Economics as a Moral Science: The Political Economy of Adam Smith* (Cheltenham, UK: Edward Elgar, 1997); James Alvey, "A Short History of Economics as a Moral Science," *Journal of Markets & Morality* 2, no. 1 (Spring 1999): 53–73; Ricardo F. Crespo, "Is Economics a Moral Science?," *Journal of Markets & Morality* 1, no. 2 (Fall 1998): 201–11; Peter J. Boettke, "Is Economics a Moral Science? A Response to Ricardo F. Crespo,"

> There are two major reasons why economics has become detached from moral concerns. First, the natural sciences came to be seen as successful, and the attempt was made to emulate that success in economics by applying natural science methods, including mathematics, to economic phenomena. Second, the self-styled economic science came to adopt positivism, which ruled out moral issues from science itself.[10]

It is the latter recognition, perhaps more than any other, that squares the revisionists off against the positivists in the debate over the prehistory of economics.

When the positivistic bias begins to be put aside and we look anew at works from earlier periods, we find the early modern era to be a rich source of intellectual ferment on economic, ethical, and legal and political topics. In the sixteenth and early seventeenth centuries, a small but influential group of theologians and jurists centered in Spain attempted to synthesize the Roman legal texts with Aristotelian and Thomistic moral philosophy. The movement began with the revival of Thomistic philosophy in Paris, where, as Camacho recounts, "Pierre Crockaert underwent an intellectual conversion from nominalist philosophy to the philosophy of Thomas Aquinas."[11]

Shortly before 1225, the year of Aquinas' birth, Aristotle's works on metaphysics, physics, politics, and ethics became available in the West, and, within the span of a generation, Aristotelianism,

---

*Journal of Markets & Morality* 1, no. 2 (Fall 1998): 212–19; and Crespo, "Is Economics a Moral Science? A Response to Peter J. Boettke," *Journal of Markets & Morality* 1, no. 2 (Fall 1998): 220–25; Jeffrey T. Young, *Economics as a Moral Science: The Political Economy of Adam Smith* (Cheltenham, UK: Edward Elgar, 1997).

10. Alvey, "A Short History of Economics as a Moral Science," 53.

11. Francisco Gómez Camacho, "Later Scholastics: Spanish Economic Thought in the Sixteenth and Seventeenth Centuries," in *Ancient and Medieval Economic Ideas and Concepts of Social Justice*, ed. S. Todd Lowry and Barry Gordon (Leiden and New York: Brill, 1998), 503.

which had been brought to Europe by Arabic scholars, would be a serious contender in medieval thought. Thomas sought a rapprochement between the Greek philosophical tradition that Aristotle represented and the Christian divine ideas tradition articulated by the likes of Augustine, pseudo-Dionysius, and Bonaventure. In 1512, Crockaert published his commentary on the last part of Thomas' *Summa theologica* with the help of a student, Francisco de Vitoria (ca. 1483–1546).[12]

Approximately two hundred years before Thomas was born, the *Corpus iuris civilis* of Justinian had been rediscovered and had become the object of academic disputation. However, the traditions of Roman law and Aristotelian and Thomistic philosophy existed in relative isolation from one other, at least until the early sixteenth century in Spain. "In the sixteenth and early seventeenth centuries," states Camacho, "a synthesis was finally achieved by that group of theologians and jurists known to historians of law as the 'late scholastics' or the 'Spanish natural law school.'"[13] Schumpeter concurs with this judgment and adds, "It is within their systems of moral theology and law that economics gained definite if not separate existence, and it is they who come nearer than does any other group to having been the 'founders' of scientific economics."[14] The Salamancans in particular, writes Moss,

12. Camacho, "Later Scholastics: Spanish Economic Thought in the Sixteenth and Seventeenth Centuries," 503.

13. Camacho, "Later Scholastics: Spanish Economic Thought in the Sixteenth and Seventeenth Centuries," 503.

14. Joseph Schumpeter, *History of Economic Analysis*, ed. Elizabeth Booty Schumpeter (Oxford: Oxford University Press, 1954), 97: "And not only that it will appear, even, that the bases they laid for a serviceable and well-integrated body of analytic tools and propositions were sounder than was much subsequent work, in the sense that a considerable part of the economics of the later nineteenth century might have been developed from those bases more quickly and with less trouble than it actually cost

> were as interested in a general theory of how exchange rates between different currencies are formed as in explaining why a bill of exchange is worth more in one region of Spain than in another region. Was the agio or exchange premium evidence of usury and therefore immoral behavior on the part of merchants and traders, or rather something 'natural' governed by the basic laws of supply and demand?[15]

The case of this so-called School of Salamanca is just one example of the rich intellectual traditions that have far too often been ignored or downplayed by contemporary scholarship. The coherent intellectual framework of Christian scholasticism reverberates not only in the field of economics but also in the related areas of ethics and law. Thus, political theorists John Neville Figgis and Otto von Gierke drew on the work of a variety of sixteenth- and seventeenth-century Dutch, Swiss, German, and Spanish jurists and ethicists who articulated concepts that laid the foundation for federalist political structures, constitutionalism, popular sovereignty, natural-law jurisprudence, and limited government in the Western legal tradition.[16] The diversity and variety of relevant sources from this period is underscored by the contribution of Protestant scholars, who produced significant scholastic works as well as more occasional treatises. Much of the early Protestant thought on economics, ethics, and law attaches to their homiletical and exegetical work in addition to the achievements in systems of moral theology and philosophy. The Dutch

to develop it, and that some of that subsequent work was therefore in the nature of a time- and labor-consuming detour."

15. Laurence S. Moss, "Introduction," in *Economic Thought in Spain: Selected Essays of Marjorie Grice-Hutchinson*, ed. Laurence S. Moss and Christopher K. Ryan (Brookfield, VT: Edward Elgar, 1993), xv.

16. On Johannes Althusius in particular, see Otto von Gierke, *The Development of Political Theory*, trans. Bernard Freyd (New York: Howard Fertig, 1966), 70; and John Neville Figgis, *Studies of Political Thought: From Gerson to Grotius, 1414–1625* (Cambridge: Cambridge University Press, 1907), 175–85.

Reformed legal thinker Johannes Althusius (1563–1638) stands as a representative example in this regard, and his contributions to the development of Western legal and political traditions are becoming increasingly appreciated.[17] After a long period in which economics, ethics, and law became detached from theology, many economists, legal scholars, political theorists, and theologians now see the benefit of studying early modern economic, ethical, and legal texts in their full cultural, often religious, context.

The Sources in Early Modern Economics, Ethics, and Law series is the latest installment in the excavation of the mines of early modern theological thought on these topics. The aim of this series is to offer economists, intellectual historians, moral theologians, and graduate students in the fields of economics, economic ethics, economic history, banking history, political economy, and moral theology a useful and accessible collection of some of the most important early modern texts in the fields of economics, ethics, and law. Now, for the first time, the unabridged texts of works such as Martín de Azpilcueta's *Commentary on the Resolution of Money* (1556), Luis de Molina's *Treatise on Money* (1597), and Juan de Mariana's *Treatise on the Alteration of Money* (1609), as well as selections from larger works such as Johannes Althusius' *Dicaeologicae* (1617) and Girolamo Zanchi's *Omnium operum theologicorum* (1619) will be available as stand-alone volumes in English translation and in modern editions with scholarly annotations. We hope that the publication of these primary texts in a series of paperbacks will help to facilitate exploration of the continuities and discontinuities,

17. See, for instance, John Witte Jr., "A Demonstrative Theory of Natural Law: The Original Contribution of Johannes Althusius," in *Public Theology for a Global Society: Essays in Honor of Max L. Stackhouse*, ed. Deirdre King Hainsworth and Scott R. Paeth (Grand Rapids: Eerdmans, 2010), 21–36; and Thomas O. Hueglin, *Early Modern Concepts for a Late Medieval World: Althusius on Community and Federalism* (Waterloo, ON: Wilfrid Laurier University Press, 1999).

agreements and disagreements, innovations and ruptures among theological communities during the latter half of the sixteenth and the early seventeenth century.

The translations and modern editions (in conjunction with the introductions by leading authorities) will show the sophistication with which Christian thinkers from a variety of confessional and theological perspectives examined issues such as the role and responsibilities of the civil magistrates, the existence and efficacy of natural law, usury, and the ethics of moneylending, as well as the new process of using bills of exchange (*cambium per litteras*) to replace the cumbersome and dangerous transportation of metallic coins between commercial fairs, which led not only to new scholastic insights on interest, credit, and international trade but also to a much more comprehensive analysis of monetary exchange and banking practices than had been undertaken before. The texts will also address the questions as particular as why the same currency was worth more in one region than another area's currency, and, moreover, why the rate of exchange fluctuated between one area and the next. These moral and economic concerns, along with many others, will be addressed in detail throughout the course of the series by some of the leading, and heretofore underappreciated, authorities from the early modern era.

# Wolfgang Musculus on Psalm 15*

*Jordan J. Ballor*

Over the last few decades, a picture of the Reformation has been formed that stands in marked contrast to the received wisdom of the early twentieth century. A history of Christian doctrine that largely emphasizes the importance of the Reformation's leading men, especially Martin Luther and John Calvin (and to a lesser extent Philipp Melanchthon and Huldrych Zwingli), has been measured and found wanting. In its place, an approach that emphasizes texts and contexts rather than archetypal paradigms has provided a more sensitive and nuanced perspective on the transition from the late medieval to the early modern period.

The work of lesser-known figures has begun to emerge from the shadows cast on the historical landscape by theologians such as Luther and Calvin. This is as true for our understanding of

---

* This introduction updates a previously published version, which included content that subsequently appeared in different places in my *Covenant, Causality, and Law: A Study in the Theology of Wolfgang Musculus* (Göttingen: Vandenhoeck & Ruprecht, 2012).

controversial doctrines such as the Lord's Supper and justification as it is for the influence of the Reformation on political, economic, and ethical thought. These minor characters of the Reformation have been found to have made major and, heretofore largely unappreciated, contributions to the developments of the Protestant Reformation and post-Reformation eras.

Wolfgang Musculus (1497–1563), a reformer in the cities of Strasbourg, Augsburg, and Bern, is one such overlooked figure. In the Anglo-American world in particular, the work of this second-generation reformer has suffered remarkable neglect. A handful of unpublished dissertations, along with only two published monographs, comprise the English-language literature focused on Musculus in the last century.[1] The bibliographic situation on the Continent is rather better, however, and the publication of an anthology commemorating the five-hundredth anniversary of Musculus' birth stands as a major recent contribution to Musculus research.[2] This present translation appears

1. Among the former are James T. Ford, "Wolfgang Musculus and the Struggle for Confessional Hegemony in Reformation Augsburg, 1531–1548" (PhD diss., University of Wisconsin–Madison, 2000); and Robert B. Ives, "The Theology of Wolfgang Musculus, 1497–1563" (PhD diss., University of Manchester, 1965). The latter are Craig S. Farmer, *The Gospel of John in the Sixteenth Century: The Johannine Exegesis of Wolfgang Musculus* (New York: Oxford University Press, 1997); and Paul Josiah Schwab, *The Attitude of Wolfgang Musculus toward Religious Tolerance* (New Haven: Yale University Press, 1933). My own previously mentioned publication, *Covenant, Causality, and Law*, along with other efforts, including this present volume, will hopefuly spark some renewed interest in Musculus. See also Scott M. Manetsch, "(Re)constructing the Pastoral Office: Wolfgang Musculus' Commentaries on 1 & 2 Corinthians," in *On the Writing of New Testament Commentaries*, ed. Stanley E. Porter and Eckhard J. Schnabel (Leiden: Brill, 2012), 253–66.

2. Rudolf Dellsperger, Rudolf Freudenberger, and Wolfgang Weber, eds. *Wolfgang Musculus (1497–1563) und die oberdeutsche Reformation* (Berlin: Akademie Verlag, 1997).

on the occasion of the four-hundred-and-fiftieth anniversary of Musculus' passing.

An example of one such underappreciated contribution by a lesser-known figure is that of Wolfgang Musculus' exegesis of Psalm 15, a text that has been foundational for the development of theological reflection on Christian righteousness and, in particular, on questions related to usury. Musculus wrote a sizeable appendix on the issue of usury for his Psalms treatise and linked it, along with another appendix on oaths, to his exegesis of Psalm 15. Musculus' appendices on oaths and usury were first translated separately from the rest of the Psalms commentary and appended to the English translation of his *Common Places* in 1563. In this way, they functioned as practical moral treatises corresponding to the larger doctrinal focus of the *Loci communes*.[3]

Each of these appendices is important in its own way for the historical development of political economy and social ethics in the Reformed tradition. They stand as predecessors to the more developed moral casuistry of the later sixteenth and seventeenth centuries. Where the first and second generations of reformers tended to address such social, political, and ethical questions in an ad hoc and occasional manner, treatments became increasingly organized and structured in the larger casuistical systems of writers such as William Perkins, William Ames, and Richard Baxter.[4]

---

3. Wolfgang Musculus, *Common Places of the Christian Religion*, trans. John Man (London: Reginalde Wolfe, 1563).

4. William Perkins, *The Whole Treatise of the Cases of Conscience* (London: John Legat, 1606); William Ames, *De conscientia et eius iure, vel casibus* (Amsterdam: I. Ianssonium, 1631). ET: *Conscience with the Power and Cases Thereof* (London: W. Christiaens, E. Griffin, J. Dawson, 1639); Richard Baxter, *A Christian Directory, or, A Summ of Practical Theology and Cases of Conscience* (London: Robert White, 1673). See also Johann Alsted, *Theologia casuum* (Hannover: Conrad Eifridum, 1621). This transition in theological reflection on moral matters corresponds to the larger movement from the early generations of the Reformation to the Reformed orthodox

Musculus' appendix on oaths takes up a question of relatively novel importance, given the contemporary challenge of more radical strands of the Reformation to such social conventions. To question the legitimacy of the oath was to challenge the entire social and political structure of the day. Musculus takes as his point of departure on this question the biblical text of Psalm 15:4, which reads in part that the righteous person is one "who swears to his neighbor and does not change."

Psalm 15:5 informs the reader that another characteristic of a righteous person is to be someone who "does not give his money for usury." In his magisterial study on the theory of usury, John T. Noonan observes, "At the same time, economics, law, theology, and ethics are all, in measure, illuminated by the history of a theory that involves them all."[5] The complex issue of usury becomes, then, a very useful device for coming to an understanding of how various interrelated themes in intellectual history have been synthesized and applied. Even more, when usury can be examined historically within an exegetical context the possibilities for fruitful analysis multiply. As David C. Steinmetz has noted, "The history of biblical interpretation is not incidental to European cultural history but central to it."[6]

---

of the later sixteenth and seventeenth centuries. See Richard A. Muller, *After Calvin: Studies in the Development of a Theological Tradition* (New York: Oxford University Press, 2003), 9–10. For a massive corresponding effort among Lutherans, see Georg Dedekenn, ed., *Thesauri Consiliorum Et Decisionum Volumen I Ecclesiastica continens* (Hamburg: Paul Lange, 1623); and Friedrich Balduin, *Tractatus Luculentus, Posthumus, Toti Reipublicæ Christianæ Utilissimus. De Materia rarissime antehac enveleata, Casibus nimirum conscientiæ* (Wittenberg: Paul Helwigius, 1628). See also Benjamin T.G. Mayes, *Counsel and Conscience: Lutheran Casuistry and Moral Reasoning after the Reformation* (Göttingen: Vandenhoeck & Ruprecht, 2011).

5. John T. Noonan Jr., *The Scholastic Analysis of Usury* (Cambridge, MA: Harvard University Press, 1957), 2.

6. David C. Steinmetz, *Luther in Context*, 2nd ed. (Grand Rapids: Baker Academic, 2002), 46.

Musculus' reflections on usury in Psalm 15 are significant because they represent a stream of Protestant thought that largely has been ignored by economic historians.[7] The preeminent significance of Calvin's thought on usury for the development of modern economics has been the subject of debate for the last century, but efforts to correct, modify, or replace the Weber thesis have tended to focus on antecedents to Calvin, whether they be Reformed (as in the case of Heinrich Bullinger) or Roman Catholic (as in the case of the school of Salamanca).[8] In contrast to Reformed thinkers such as Calvin, Bullinger, and Bucer who modified to a greater or lesser extent the received theological perspectives on usury, Musculus represents the continuing vitality of a more restrictive, less permissive approach to these questions.

While not often found worthy of independent study, there are two areas in particular in which the work of Wolfgang Musculus has often been noticed by the secondary scholarship. The first is in the complicated history of what has become known as "covenant" or "federal" theology. In his *Loci communes*, initially pub-

7. Max Weber, *The Protestant Ethic and the Spirit of Capitalism*, trans. Talcott Parsons (New York: Routledge, 2006); R. H. Tawney, *Religion and the Rise of Capitalism: A Historical Study* (London: John Murray, 1960); and more recently Rosa-Maria Gelpi and François Julien-Labruyère, *The History of Consumer Credit: Doctrines and Practices*, trans. M. L. Gavin (London: Macmillan, 2000). For a study focusing on Luther, Zwingli, and Calvin, see Ernest Ramp, *Das Zinsproblem. Eine historische Untersuchung* (Zurich: Zwingli-Verlag, 1949). For a study that surveys the opinion of a variety of reformers and concludes that the disagreements are merely terminological and superficial, see Eric Kerridge, *Usury, Interest and the Reformation* (Burlington, VT: Ashgate, 2002).

8. On Bullinger, see J. Wayne Baker, "Heinrich Bullinger and the Idea of Usury," *Sixteenth Century Journal* 5, no. 1 (April 1974): 49–70. See also Guenther H. Haas, *The Concept of Equity in Calvin's Ethics* (Carlisle: Paternoster, 1997), especially 117–21. On the Salamancans in particular, see Stephen J. Grabill, ed., *Sourcebook in Late-Scholastic Monetary Theory: The Contributions of Martin de Azpilcueta, Luis de Molina, S.J., and Juan de Mariana, S.J.* (Lanham, MD: Lexington, 2007).

lished in 1560, Wolfgang Musculus was perhaps the first reformer to grant the topic of covenant a separate treatment within the context of a major systematic contribution to sixteenth-century Reformed theology.[9] When nineteenth-century writers proposed covenant as a seventeenth-century alternative to the perceived central dogma of predestinarian Calvinistic theology, a discussion arose regarding the predecessors to the developments in covenant thought from Zacharius Ursinus (1534–1583) to Johannes Coccius (1603–1669). These discussions have taken some note of Musculus' importance in the formation of covenantal thinking in Reformed theology. A characteristic feature of Musculus' treatment of covenant in the *Loci* is his distinction between general and special covenants. The significance of Musculus' doctrinal formulation of a *foedus generale*, and whether or not it is a forerunner of the so-called covenant of works, has been a subject of some controversy in the secondary literature.[10]

9. See Wolfgang Musculus, "De foedere ac testamento Dei," in *Loci communes in usus sacrae Theologiae candidatorum parati* (Basel: Johannes Herwagen, 1564), 141–46. On Musculus' *Loci*, see especially Herman J. Selderhuis, "Die Loci Communes des Wolfgang Musculus: Reformierte Dogmatik anno 1560," in *Wolfgang Musculus (1497–1563) und die oberdeutsche Reformation*, 311–30.

10. Heinrich Heppe, *Geschichte des Pietismus und der Mystik in der reformirten Kirche, namentlich der Niederlande* (Leiden: Brill, 1879), 208; Gottlob Schrenk, *Gottesreich und Bund im alteren Protestantismus, vornehmlich bei Johannes Coccejus. Zugleich ein Beitrag zur Geschichte des Pietismus und der heilsgeschichtlichen Theologie* (Gutersloh: Bertelsmann, 1923), 50; Karl Barth, *Die Kirchliche Dogmatik*, vol. 4, pt. 1 (Zurich: Evangelischer Verlag, 1953), 57. ET: *Church Dogmatics*, Volume 4: *The Doctrine of God, Part 1* (Edinburgh: T. & T. Clark, 2004), 55; Holmes Rolston III, *John Calvin versus the Westminster Confession* (Richmond: John Knox, 1972), 12; William K. B. Stoever, *A Faire and Easie Way to Heaven: Covenant Theology and Antinomianism in Early Massachusetts* (Middletown, CT: Wesleyan University Press, 1978), 215n4; R. T. Kendall, *Calvin and English Calvinism to 1649* (Oxford: Oxford University Press, 1979), 39n2; J. Wayne Baker, *Heinrich Bullinger and the Covenant: The Other Reformed Tradition* (Athens: Ohio University Press, 1980), 201; Robert Letham, "The *Foedus Operum*:

Indeed, Musculus' covenantal thought provides an important interpretive context for his discussion of oaths.

A second major set of references to Musculus note his importance in the history of biblical exegesis. Pierre Bayle called Musculus "one of the most celebrated Divines of the sixteenth century," but also opined that "if his works were of great advantage to the Protestant party, as no doubt they were," that by Bayle's own time "they were no longer so, for people have for a long time left off reading them."[11] Despite Bayle's judgment, there is some evidence of Musculus' ongoing influence, not only through his *Loci communes*, but also through his numerous and massive biblical commentaries. A modern commentator has observed that Musculus "in many ways set the sixteenth-century standard for thorough exegesis," and this judgment is borne out by the appropriation of his work in following generations.[12] Musculus

Some Factors Accounting for Its Development," *Sixteenth Century Journal* 14, no. 4 (Winter 1983): 462–63; Stephen Strehle, *Calvinism, Federalism, and Scholasticism: A Study of the Reformed Doctrine of Covenant* (New York: Peter Lang, 1988), 157; David A. Weir, *The Origins of Federal Theology in Sixteenth-Century Reformation Thought* (New York: Oxford University Press, 1990), 12; Charles S. McCoy and J. Wayne Baker, *Fountainhead of Federalism: Heinrich Bullinger and the Covenantal Tradition* (Louisville: Westminster/John Knox, 1991), 140–41n20; and Lyle D. Bierma, *German Calvinism in the Confessional Age: The Covenant Theology of Caspar Olevianus* (Grand Rapids: Baker Academic, 1996), 62.

11. Pierre Bayle, *Dictionaire historique et critique*, vol. 10, new ed. (Paris: Desoer, 1820), s.v. "Musculus (Wolfgang)," 584, 588nF. ET: *A General Dictionary, Historical and Critical*, vol. 7, trans. John Peter Bernard, Thomas Birch, John Lockman, et al. (London: James Bettenbam, 1738), s.v. "Musculus (Wolfgang)," 698, 700nF. For biographical information, Bayle largely relies on Melchior Adam, *Vitae Germanorum Theologorum* (Heidelberg: Geydes, 1620).

12. Mickey L. Mattox, *Defender of the Most Holy Matriarchs: Martin Luther's Interpretation of the Women of Genesis in the* Ennarationes in Genesin, *1535–1545* (Leiden: Brill, 2003), 278. Farmer judges that Musculus "belongs among the elite group of the premiere biblical scholars of the sixteenth century." See Craig S. Farmer, "Musculus, Wolfgang (1497–1563)," in

is cited directly by writers as diverse as Jacob Arminius, Peter Bulkeley, Edmund Calamy (the elder), Edward Fisher, Johann Gerhard, Hugo Grotius, Michael Hawke, and Herman Witsius in the seventeenth century, as well as Petrus Brouwer, John Gill, and Hermann Venema in the eighteenth.[13]

Musculus' facility with the biblical languages, foundational for his exegetical work, was achieved relatively late in life.[14] During

---

*Dictionary of Major Biblical Interpreters*, ed. Donald K. McKim (Downers Grove: IVP Academic, 2007), 768.

13. Jacob Arminius, "Dissertation on the True and Genuine Sense of the Seventh Chapter of the Epistle to the Romans," in *The Works of James Arminius*, trans. James Nichols, vol. 2., London ed. (Grand Rapids: Baker, 1991), 531, 574, 590, 627–29; Peter Bulkeley, *The Gospel-Covenant; or The Covenant of Grace Opened* (London: Benjamin Allen, 1646), 18; Edmund Calamy, *The Godly Mans Ark, or, City of Refuge in the Day of His Distresse* (London: Jo. Hancock, 1657), Sermon I, Psalm 119:92, pp. 4–5; Edward Fisher, *The Marrow of Modern Divinity: Touching both the Covenant of Works, and the Covenant of Grace* (London: G. Calvert, 1645), 6–7, 15, 16–17, 67, 121, 123; Johann Gerhard, *Theological Commonplaces: On the Nature of God and on the Trinity*, trans. Richard J. Dinda, ed. Benjamin T. G. Mayes (St. Louis: Concordia, 2007), loc. 2, sec. 179, p. 174; Hugo Grotius, *Ordinum Hollandia ac Westfrisiae Pietas (1613)*, trans. and ed. Edwin Rabbi (Leiden: Brill, 1995), sec. 133, p. 199; idem, *De imperio summarum potestatum circa sacra*, vol. 1, trans. and ed. Harm-Jan van Dam (Leiden: Brill, 2001), 1.8.169; 10.27.511; Michael Hawke, *Killing Is Murder, and No Murder* (London: Mich. Hawke, 1657), 28; Herman Witsius, *The Economy of the Covenants Between God and Man*, trans. William Crookshank (London: R. Baynes, 1822), 1.1.6.7.109; 2.4.7.5.234; 2.4.7.24.242; Petrus Brouwer, *De XXVste Psalm, in eene Doorgaande Verklaaring* (Dordrecht: Pieter van Braam, 1769), 7nA, 77nA; John Gill, *Complete Body of Doctrinal and Practical Divinity*, 2 vols. (Grand Rapids: Baker, 1978), 2.5.637; Hermann Venema, *Commentarius ad Psalmos CXI–CL*, vol. 6 (Leeuwarden: H. A. de Chalmot, 1767), 278, 517.

14. The most thorough modern treatment of Musculus' life is the portrait by Rudolf Dellsperger, "Wolfgang Musculus (1497–1563) Leben und Werk," in *Wolfgang Musculus (1497–1563) und die oberdeutsche Reformation*, 23–36. See also the sketch in Farmer, *The Gospel of John in the Sixteenth Century*, 6–8; and the treatment in Ives, "The Theology of Wolfgang Musculus,"

his time spent as a Benedictine in the Lixheim cloister in the area west of Strasbourg, Musculus became known as "the Lutheran monk" for his advocacy of Protestant doctrine. It was after his departure from the monastery in 1527 that Musculus came to Strasbourg, eventually working as a clerk for Martin Bucer. Here, Musculus undertook the study of Hebrew, Aramaic, and Greek while attending theological lectures given by Bucer and Wolfgang Capito.[15] After a period as a preacher in neighboring towns, Musculus was sent to the imperial city of Augsburg in 1531. He would be a leading pastor in Augsburg for the next two decades, promoting the cause of the Reformed faction in contest with the Lutheran and Roman Catholic parties. In 1548, at the imposition of the Augsburg Interim, Musculus and his family fled the city, eventually finding temporary refuge in Zurich. Musculus opted to remain in Zurich until he was offered a position in Bern, but Craig S. Farmer relates that during this period after his flight from Augsburg, "largely on the basis of his reputation as a skilled commentator, Musculus received numerous offers to assume teaching posts throughout Europe."[16] Musculus took up the professorship in theology at the school in Bern in 1549, a position he held until his death in 1563.[17]

In addition to various tracts, sermons, catechisms, and treatises published occasionally throughout his career, such as a

---

3–106. See also Reinhard Bodenmann, *Wolfgang Musculus (1497–1563), Destin d'un Autodidacte Lorrain au Siècle des Réformes* (Geneva: Droz, 2000), which includes a critical edition and French translation of the major biographical document on Musculus from the sixteenth century, the *Vita Wolfgangi Musculi* written by his son Abraham Musculus.

15. See also, Bodenmann, *Wolfgang Musculus (1497–1563)*, 369–77.

16. Farmer, *The Gospel of John in the Sixteenth Century*, 4. See also, Bodenmann, *Wolfgang Musculus (1497–1563)*, 393–403.

17. On the school in Bern, see Beat Immenhauser, "'Hohe Schule' oder Universität? Zur Pfarrerausbildung in Bern im 16. Jahrhundert," in *Politics and Reformations: Communities, Polities, Nations, and Empires*, ed. Christopher Ocker et al. (Leiden: Brill, 2007), 143–78.

polemical dispute regarding the Mass with the Roman Catholic theologian Johannes Cochläus, Musculus produced works of three major types: (1) editions and translations of Patristic texts, (2) biblical commentaries, and (3) his *Loci communes*.[18] Of particular importance are Musculus' biblical commentaries, which he began during his Augsburg period with the publication of his commentary on Matthew in 1544.[19] Following the publication of his commentary on John in two parts (in 1545 and 1548), Musculus produced a commentary on the Psalms in 1551.[20] For the remainder of his life, Musculus would continue to work on biblical exegesis, publishing on the Decalogue (1553); Genesis (1554); Romans (1555); Isaiah (1557); 1 and 2 Corinthians (1559); Galatians and Ephesians (1561); and Philippians, Colossians, 1 and 2 Thessalonians, and 1 Timothy (published posthumously in 1565).

18. His response to an attack by Cochläus was published in Latin, *Adversus libellum Iohannis Cochlaei de Sacerdotio ac Sacrifico novae legis aeditum* (Augsburg: Philipp Ulhardt, 1544); and later in German, *Auff das Büchlin Johannes Cochlei welches er zur verthädigung Bäpstlichs Priesterthumbs vnnd Meßopffers im Jar 1544* (Augsburg: Philipp Ulhardt, 1545). For more on Musculus and Cochläus, see Heribert Smolinsky, "Wolfgang Musculus und die Römisch Kirche: der Streit mit Johannes Cochläus," in *Wolfgang Musculus (1497–1563) und die oberdeutsche Reformation*, 173–87. A thorough bibliography of various editions and translations of Musculus' works is available by Marc van Wijnkoop Lüthi, "Druckwerkeverzeichnis des Wolfgang Musculus (1497–1563)," in *Wolfgang Musculus (1497–1563) und die oberdeutsche Reformation*, 351–414.

19. Wolfgang Musculus, *In Evang. Matthaevm Commentarii* (Basel: Johannes Herwagen, 1544).

20. For Musculus' commentary on John, see Farmer, *The Gospel of John in the Sixteenth Century*. While in Augsburg, Musculus worked on his Psalms commentary, which was published after he came to Bern as *In Sacrosanctum Dauidis Psalterium Comentarij* (Basel: Johannes Herwagen, 1551).

## The Psalms Commentary

Musculus' commentary on the Psalms is his largest exegetical work, running to roughly eleven hundred folio pages in the various editions (a count that does not include the two appendices on oaths and usury). The commentary was one of Musculus' most popular, going through six Latin editions by the end of the century along with another published in 1618. Portions of the commentary, whether the exegesis of selected psalms or the appendices, were published in German, Dutch, French, and English throughout the sixteenth century.[21] In 1646, Edward Leigh would include Musculus, along with Heinrich Möller (Mollerus), Simeon de Muis, and John Calvin, among his list of "the best Expositors on the Psalms."[22]

The commentary is dedicated to the Bernese authorities and follows Musculus' regular exegetical pattern. Before each psalm, Musculus provides a brief *argumentum*, or summary, of the text. He then produces the biblical text of the psalm, broken up into

21. See, for instance, Musculus, *Den eersten Psalm Davids, seer fijn ende Christleick wtgheleit* (Emden: E. van der Erve; Gailliart, 1554); idem, *Vom Woker* (Rostock: Ludwig Dietz, 1554); idem, *Een claere ende Scriftelicke onderrichtinghe vanden Eedt* (n.p.: Martin Micron, 1555); idem, *On the Lawful and Unlawful Usury Amongest Christians* (n.p.: ca. 1556); idem, *Traicté de l'usure* (n.p.: 1557); idem, *An Exposition of the 51 Psalmen by Musculus translated* (London: 1586); idem, *Von dem schandlichen hochschaedlichen, von Gott verfluchten unnd verdampten, by heutiger Welt aber hochgeehrtem, gemehrtem unnd allen Geytzhaelsen ausserwoehlten Schaetzlein dem Wucher so welandt* (Strasbourg: Jobins Erben, 1593).

22. Edward Leigh, *A Treatise of Divinity* (London: E. Griffin, 1646), 1.3.55. Leigh also prefers Musculus on Matthew, John, and 2 Corinthians. Richard Bernard had previously recommended the *Common Places* and commentaries of Musculus. See Richard Bernard, *The Faithfull Shepheard* (London: Arnold Harfield, 1607), 40. For his part, Calvin acknowledges the value of Musculus' Psalms commentary, noting that Musculus "in the judgment of good men, has earned no small praise by his diligence and industry in this walk." See John Calvin, *Commentary on the Book of Psalms*, vol. 1, trans. James Anderson (Grand Rapids: Eerdmans, 1949), xxxv.

shorter pericopes where he judges appropriate. The main body of exegesis itself consists of three parts: the reading (*lectio*); the explanation (*explanatio*); and the observations (*observatio*).[23]

The reading consists of Musculus' exploration of alternative and variant textual readings, drawing on "Hebrew, Septuagint, Vulgate, and patristic renderings of selected lemmata."[24] In the Psalms commentary, the reading for the entire pericope is placed before the explanations and the observations. Musculus then proceeds verse by verse, first giving the explanation for the verse, and, on that basis, making his observations. In the observations, Musculus "discusses the moral maxims that may be derived from the text."[25] In this way, there is a methodological progression from establishing the text in the reading, understanding the text through the explanation, and finally applying the text in the observation. It is with this structure in mind that Farmer judges Musculus' commentaries to be "dominated by tropological exposition," and Musculus' concern to connect the biblical text to practical application is apparent in this selection from his Psalms commentary.[26]

## Psalm 15

One benefit of placing Musculus' appendices on oaths and usury within the broader exegetical context, specifically his comments on Psalm 15, is that it allows us to better understand how doctrine emerges from and is shaped by exegesis. As we have seen, Musculus' exegetical method builds from text to application, from the *lectio*, to the *explanatio*, to the *observatio*. In the decade prior

---

23. This tripartite structure is standard for Musculus. In the Genesis commentary, Musculus would add a fourth section, *quaestio*, to fill out his exegesis, but this category would generally be omitted in later commentaries. See Farmer, *The Gospel of John in the Sixteenth Century*, 200n21.

24. Farmer, *The Gospel of John in the Sixteenth Century*, 200n21.

25. Farmer, *The Gospel of John in the Sixteenth Century*, 50.

26. Farmer, *The Gospel of John in the Sixteenth Century*, 50.

to the publication of his *Loci communes* in 1560, Musculus was heavily engaged in writing biblical commentaries, and we can see how this plays out in the composition of his Common Places. These *Loci communes* function not only as common topics, in the sense of the usual and standard issues to be discussed in a systematic theological presentation, but also as Common Places in Scripture where these discussions are rooted. Put quite starkly, Musculus' doctrinal formulations cannot be fully understood without engagement of the exegetical background within which they were formed.

Psalm 15 presents just such a context for the questions regarding oaths and usury. Controversy over oaths was a relatively new phenomenon in the sixteenth century, but the discussion of usury, focused particularly on Psalm 15, goes back to the earliest conversations in the church. As Noonan writes, "Both because it admits no exceptions and because of its use by the first ecumenical council," this Psalm in particular "becomes the favorite early medieval biblical text against usury."[27] Indeed, there is typically more than one scriptural text within a series that function as "seats of doctrine" (*sedes doctrinae*) for Reformed orthodox theological constructions.[28] Sensitivity to this prevents

27. Noonan, *The Scholastic Analysis of Usury*, 15. The popularity of this text and topic continues into the early modern era. In addition to Musculus' exegetical treatment, see Urban Rhegius, *Der XV. Psalm Dauids* (Magdeburg: Michael Lotther, 1537); and George Downame, *Lectures on the XV. Psalme* (London: Adam Islip, 1604).

28. See Richard A. Muller, *Post-Reformation Reformed Dogmatics: The Rise and Development of Reformed Orthodoxy, ca. 1520 to ca. 1725*, 4 vols. (Grand Rapids: Baker Academic, 2003), 1:87. See also Richard A. Muller, *After Calvin*, 58–60; and idem, *The Unaccommodated Calvin: Studies in the Foundation of a Theological Tradition* (New York: Oxford University Press, 2000), 107.

the reader from making greater claims about the theological tradition attached to a single biblical text than is warranted.[29]

Moreover, attention to the commentary on a biblical text allows us to more carefully compare a text *sui generis*, placing a particular writer's comments within the broader history of exegesis. If we examine the position of John Calvin as expressed in his Psalms commentary, for instance, to that of Wolfgang Musculus, we see a marked contrast in both style and attitude. Where Musculus opposes all forms of usury, Calvin briefly and handily dispenses with a straightforward application of the Psalms text. Calvin contends that the prohibition against usury was a ceremonial law pointing toward the principle of equity and only prohibited usurious lending to the poor. "We know," writes Calvin, "that generally it is not the rich who are exhausted by their usury, but poor men, who ought rather to be relieved."[30] If only we would follow "the rule of equity," says Calvin, "it would not be necessary to enter into lengthened disputes concerning usury."[31] It is this "common principle of justice" to which Cal-

29. Benjamin Nelson, for instance, focuses primarily on the exegesis of Deuteronomy 23:20–21, another important biblical text for theological reflection on usury, as the basis for a grand narrative of the "transvaluation of values" from "brotherhood" to "otherhood." Without broader engagement with other scriptural texts, such as Psalm 15:5, as well as systematic and polemical treatises, valid comprehensive interpretations of the doctrinal development of usury cannot be made. See Benjamin Nelson, *The Idea of Usury: From Tribal Brotherhood to Universal Otherhood*, 2nd ed. (Chicago: University of Chicago Press, 1969), 19.

30. Calvin, *Commentary on the Book of Psalms*, 1:213. For a brief comparison of the exegetical method of Calvin and Musculus related to the formation of their respective doctrinal systems, see Muller, *The Unaccommodated Calvin*, 112–13. Calvin's commentary style, emphasizing *facilitas* and *brevitas*, is exhibited in his treatment of usury in this Psalm and belies the argument of Kerridge that Calvin was "forced to resort to long-winded circumlocution" in defining usury. See Kerridge, *Usury, Interest and the Reformation*, 30.

31. Calvin, *Commentary on the Book of Psalms*, 1:214.

vin refers that is operative for applying the Psalms text in the Christian era. As Herman Selderhuis writes, "Calvin believes that receiving a gain from charging interest is perfectly lawful when it does not injure anyone."[32]

The key context that the full exegesis of Psalm 15 provides is the interpretive emphasis on Christian righteousness. Musculus makes a distinction between the dispensations of the Old and New Testaments, urging his reader to obedience by asking rhetorically, "For which of the faithful is ignorant of the fact that a zeal for piety and righteousness ought to be preeminent in us, who do not dwell in a shadowy tabernacle and mount but in the kingdom of the Son of God, and who have been transported into that truth?"[33] Here, we have an emphasis common to Reformed commentators of the early modern era, a contrast between the "shadows" of the Old Testament and the "light" of the New Testament. This is a hermeneutical theme that recurs throughout Musculus' work and Reformed exegesis more generally.[34] However, where Calvin argues that the prohibition of usury was a part of the shadows of the law that passes away in the New Testament, Musculus uses the shift to argue from the lesser to the greater. Because usury was prohibited among the Old Testament community, it ought to be despised that much more among Christians.

This greater "zeal for piety and righteousness" among Christians is contrasted not only with the situation of God's people in the Old Testament, but also with those who are not part of the covenant community. The contrast between a form of civil or

32. Herman J. Selderhuis, *Calvin's Theology of the Psalms* (Grand Rapids: Baker Academic, 2007), 200.

33. Musculus, *On Righteousness, Oaths, and Usury*, 8.

34. See the discussion "De discrimine veteris & novi Testamenti" in Musculus, *Loci communes*, 146–47. See also Muller, *Post-Reformation Reformed Dogmatics*, 2:493–97.

public good and Christian righteousness is manifest as Musculus summarizes the Psalm's import in verse 2:

> The chief point that must be observed is that kind of righteousness that the prophet prescribes to those who would remain inhabitants of the tabernacle and holy mountain of God. He clearly requires that sort of righteousness from those people that does not exist in the ceremonies and legal shadows only, but that embraces the whole life and also lives and breathes true honesty of soul and charity toward one's neighbor.[35]

This distinction between types of goods, reflected variously in ecclesiastical and civil realms, becomes an important part of Musculus' analysis of usury and the relevance of its application in positive law.

The key distinction for Musculus between the realities of Christian righteousness and civil morality are the conditions of the special covenant first explicitly enjoined to Abraham: "Walk before me and be blameless."[36] Farmer has noted the tropological, or moral, emphasis of Musculus' exegesis, and this point comes through clearly where Musculus contends, "A true zeal for righteousness is not found in a bare knowledge alone, but is located in its practice. We do not reject knowledge, but we require the sort that is living and effective. For a pious person, to know righteousness is not simply to know what it is, but to press it out into one's deeds."[37]

In verse 3, Musculus notes that the Psalmist transitions from "a summary of righteousness of words and deeds" to the examination of "certain kinds" of righteousness, a move from the general to the particular. Thus, the concluding verses concerning oaths and usury outline particular forms of righteousness.

---

35. Musculus, *On Righteousness, Oaths, and Usury*, 9–10.
36. Musculus, *On Righteousness, Oaths, and Usury*, 11.
37. Musculus, *On Righteousness, Oaths, and Usury*, 12.

One other item to note beyond the context of a distinction between Christian and other forms of righteousness is Musculus' definition of Christian social responsibility. Musculus exhorts, "Let each person consider in what way he may accomplish righteousness: first, toward persons in general; next, toward those to whom he is especially connected."[38] This approach is reflective of a nascent appreciation of the complexity and diversity of social relations, what would become a hallmark emphasis in Reformed ethical and political thought. Musculus defines a neighbor as "someone who is bound to us at some point, either by religion, humanity, blood, affinity, friendship, either in familiar or civil society; or by proximity, or conjoined to us by some plight of necessity. God has mutually conjoined us together in many degrees, so that there are also many occasions for this hand of love and beneficence."[39]

This perspective has implications for Musculus' political thought as expressed in his explication of verse 4 dealing with the oath. Musculus' view is part of a strand of Reformed thinking that holds the role of the Christian magistrate as critical to the imposition of discipline in the church. In concord with his emphasis on the true zeal for righteousness working itself out in deeds, Musculus writes, "the fear of God is not only in those things that immediately concern God (that is, the first table of the Decalogue), but also in those things that pertain to one's neighbor."[40] The vertical aspect of the first-table commandments

---

38. Musculus, *On Righteousness, Oaths, and Usury*, 12.

39. Musculus, *On Righteousness, Oaths, and Usury*, 26. Compare with Augustine, *Teaching Christianity: De Doctrina Christiana*, trans. Edmund Hill, part 1, vol. 11, *The Works of Saint Augustine: A Translation for the Twenty-first Century* (New York: New City Press, 1996), 1.28.29.118: "All people are to be loved equally; but since you cannot be of service to everyone, you have to take greater care of those who are more closely joined to you by a turn, so to say, of fortune's wheel, whether by occasion of place or time, or any other such circumstance."

40. Musculus, *On Righteousness, Oaths, and Usury*, 33.

intersect with the second-table commandments in the person of the Christian magistrate: "In our time, we think that if a pious man and citizen of the kingdom of God should keep good faith with his neighbor, whoever he may be, then how much more should he keep good faith with his magistrate, and next, besides that, how much more fully with the Lord God?"[41]

In his exegesis of verse 5, Musculus lays out in summary form his position on usury that will be explicated more fully in the appendix. He finds that the loaning of money "if done rightly, is a kind of true kindness. However, if it should approach usury, then the kindness is perverted into viciousness."[42] Musculus' alignment with the older medieval rejection of usury is signified in his formulation that "the farmer who commits his seed to the ground for interest (*usura*) does not sin. However, whoever gives his money to his neighbor for interest does sin."[43]

## The Appendix on Oaths

As noted previously, of the two questions Musculus treats with extended treatises, the problem of oaths represents a comparatively new issue for debate, at least when contrasted to the centuries-long discussion over usury that had preceded the sixteenth century.[44] The basic context that gives rise to discussion of the issue in the early modern era is the challenge to the validity of the oath by various parties of the so-called radical

41. Musculus, *On Righteousness, Oaths, and Usury*, 35.

42. Musculus, *On Righteousness, Oaths, and Usury*, 37–38.

43. Musculus, *On Righteousness, Oaths, and Usury*, 38.

44. For a discussion of kinds of oaths in the seventeenth century, see Conal Condren, *Argument and Authority in Early Modern England: The Presupposition of Oaths and Offices* (Cambridge: Cambridge University Press, 2006), 233–53. See also John Spurr, "A Profane History of Early Modern Oaths," *Transactions of the Royal Historical Society*, Sixth Series, 11 (2001): 37–63; and Helen Silving, "The Oath: I," *Yale Law Journal* 68, no. 7 (June 1959): 1329–90.

Reformation, movements dubbed "Anabaptist" or "Catabaptist" by their adversaries. Musculus says of his treatment of the oath, "This question would not be necessary if the Anabaptists in our time had not thrown the consciences of many into confusion by that erroneous doctrine by which they strive to destroy absolutely every oath from the public, as if oaths were illicit."[45] A representative statement of Anabaptist consensus appears in the seventh point of the Schleitheim Articles of 1527: "All swearing has been forbidden because we cannot fulfill what is promised in swearing." Following this judgment, the article attempts to answer various challenges to this understanding of "God's simple command" contained in Matthew 5:33–37.[46]

In a recent article examining three Reformation-era polemics against the Anabaptist view, Farmer introduces the text that would be foundational for Musculus' later appendix on oaths. Farmer notes that Musculus' *Peaceful and Christian Dialogue*, first published in the vernacular German in 1533 in Augsburg, was later modified from a dialogue "into an essay on the oath, which he included in his Psalm Commentary of 1551."[47] With the advent of the Reformation, radical groups would raise new challenges to doctrines and practices, such as the oath, that were accepted among Lutherans, Roman Catholics, and Reformed alike.

In order to properly understand Musculus' view of the oath, it is necessary to place his opinion within the broader context

45. Musculus, *On Righteousness, Oaths, and Usury*, 45.

46. Michael Sattler, "The Schleitheim Articles," in *The Radical Reformation*, trans. and ed. Michael G. Baylor (Cambridge: Cambridge University Press, 1991), 178.

47. Craig S. Farmer, "Reformation-Era Polemics Against Anabaptist Oath Refusal," *Mennonite Quarterly Review* 81 (April 2007): 212. Musculus' original work is *Ain frydsams unnd Christlichs Gesprech ains Evangelischen auff ainer und ains Widerteüffers auff der andern seyten so sy des Aydschwürs halben mitainander thünd* (Augsburg: Philip Ulhardt, 1533).

of his theology, particularly with regard to two related topics: covenants and vows.

Musculus' mature statement on the topic of covenant appears in his *Loci communes*, but the essential basis of this statement is present in his commentary on Genesis. The focus of Musculus' construal of the covenant is to place emphasis on the divine initiative. In his locus *De fœdere ac testamento Dei*, Musculus insists that it is entirely astounding that God in his infinite majesty, whose will and power is most free, considers it worthy to bind and obligate himself to the rule of covenants or pacts, out of neither necessity to act nor hope for any other advantage.[48] Why then does God deign to bind himself in this way? "So that through these two immovable things," writes Musculus alluding to Hebrews 6:17–18, "promise and oath, because it is impossible for God to lie, we might have a most strong refuge to which we might flee in all temptations, and we might continuously seek to strengthen the keeping of our hope to the end."[49] It is purely for our benefit that God graciously makes clear his firm purposes in covenantal relationships. Musculus' emphasis on the presence of covenantal oaths helps distinguish a bare promise from a covenantal obligation. A covenant is identified by the presence not merely of promise but also by the binding of oaths (*iureiurandum*). Covenants function as divine institutions intended to provide comfort for God's people.

Vows, conversely, are human institutions directed toward God. Where a covenant is a promise from God combined with an oath, a vow is a human promise "piously and righteously

48. Musculus, *Loci communes*, 142.

49. Musculus, *Loci communes*, 142: "… ut per duas res immobiles, promissionem ac iusiurandum, quandoquidem impossibile est mentiri Deum, solatium habeamus omnium fortissimum, ad quod in omnibus tentationibus confugiamus, speique nostrae ad finem usque retinendae corroborationem quaeramus."

made to God."[50] In some sense, then, covenants and vows are reciprocal realities. The former are made from God to humans, and the latter are made from humans to God. This correspondence is critical in distinguishing a vow (*votum*) from an oath (*iureiurandum*). The distinction is made clear in that it is not "licit to vow, except to God alone. But we may swear to man, and bind ourselves to him by an oath."[51] The corresponding realities of covenants and vows form the primarily vertical dimensions that orient the proper use of oaths.

Thus, where covenants and vows primarily concern the divine-human relationship, oaths lend stability and certainty to human interrelations. Musculus observes, "By taking an oath, those things that are doubtful and uncertain are confirmed. Also, if something arises that is disputed, it is settled by the intervention of an oath."[52] Musculus points not only to the observable benefits of oaths in society, but also to the scriptural affirmation of the practice. He writes, "Therefore, the use of oath-taking has been commended not only in such a way by its quality, but also by the commandment of God, so that it is a fanatical person who wishes to remove it as if he is destroying a reprehensible thing from the community and wishes to cut off things that calm human affairs."[53]

Musculus' opposition to the Anabaptist rejection of oaths is in part, therefore, based on suspicion that acceptance and implementation of the Anabaptist view would radically upset the world order. After rehearsing the positive role that the legitimate oath plays in social life, Musculus asks rhetorically, "Who is the sort

50. Musculus, *Loci communes*, 568: "Propria tamen significatio vocis huius est, qua promissionem significat, eamque non quamlibet, sed Deo religiose ac sanctè factam."

51. Musculus, *Loci communes*, 571: "Vovere non licet nisi Deo soli: iurare verò possumus homini, illlique; nos iureiurando reddere obstrictos."

52. Musculus, *On Righteousness, Oaths, and Usury*, 44.

53. Musculus, *On Righteousness, Oaths, and Usury*, 49.

of person who does not see that the advantage of an oath is so great that it cannot be withdrawn from human affairs without great detriment?"[54] For Musculus, as for many of the Reformers, the Anabaptist is just such a person.[55]

The immediate scriptural occasion for the context, Psalm 15:4, affirms the use of oaths. Indeed, as noted previously, this psalm describes the necessary "kind of integrity from a citizen of the kingdom of God," including that he does not wish to change "what he swore to his neighbor."[56] Moving from the Old Testament affirmation of oaths, Musculus engages the core argument from the command of Christ that "you shall not swear at all."[57] Musculus proceeds to examine the circumstances within which an oath might be either legitimate or illegitimate, and concludes that Christ had only illegitimate oaths in view.

Indeed, Christ did not prohibit legitimate oaths, used in legal, economic, or religious contexts, but simply "the usual ones used in conversation."[58] The interpretive move Musculus makes is thus from the approval given to oaths in the Old Testament to a nuanced and careful clarification of what Christ's apparent blanket injunction against oath-swearing means in the New Testament. As Farmer rightly notes, "Musculus recognized the Anabaptist challenge on this particular issue—the question of oath swearing—as fundamentally a hermeneutical challenge."[59]

---

54. Musculus, *On Righteousness, Oaths, and Usury*, 48.

55. One place where the Reformed tradition explicitly identifies Anabaptism with anarchism comes in Article 36 of the Belgic Confession as modified in 1566. On the revision of this article see, Nicolaas H. Gootjes, *The Belgic Confession: Its History and Sources* (Grand Rapids: Baker Academic, 2007), 127–31.

56. Musculus, *On Righteousness, Oaths, and Usury*, 43.

57. Musculus, *On Righteousness, Oaths, and Usury*, 45.

58. Musculus, *On Righteousness, Oaths, and Usury*, 62.

59. Farmer, "Reformation-Era Polemics Against Anabaptist Oath Refusal," 213.

## The Appendix on Usury

In contrast with the question of oaths, in the sixteenth century there were long-standing debates and doctrinal statements on the question of usury. Musculus affirms what he believes to be the traditional definition of usury as "not only the reception, but also the hope and expectation for something beyond your principal," and in which more is received "beyond what has been given."[60] Whereas the Anabaptist challenge to the legitimacy of the oath is the immediate context for Musculus' defense of the oath, the confessional strife among various Protestant factions on the one hand, and Roman Catholics on the other, forms the proximate polemical background for Musculus' discussion of usury.

In 1515, at the instigation of Conrad Peutinger, the town clerk in Augsburg, Johann Eck wrote a treatise defending the so-called triple contract, a business agreement favored by banking houses such as the Fuggers that was designed to insure a guaranteed rate of return (in this case 5 percent).[61] In that same year, Eck traveled to Bologna to dispute the question at the university.

---

60. Musculus, *On Righteousness, Oaths, and Usury*, 81.

61. On the triple contract, see Noonan, *The Scholastic Idea of Usury*, 202–29, especially 208–12, which focuses on Eck and his treatise, *Tractatus de contractu quinque de centum* (1515). For background on Eck's defense, see Steven W. Rowan, "Ulrich Zasius and John Eck: 'Faith Need Not be Kept with an Enemy'," *Sixteenth Century Journal* 8, no. 2 (1977): 87–88. See also Heiko A. Oberman, *Masters of the Reformation* (Cambridge: Cambridge University Press, 1981), 128–57. On the Fuggers, see Richard Ehrenberg, *Das Zeitalter der Fugger*, 2 vols. (Jena: Gustav Fischer, 1922); ET: *Capital and Finance in the Age of the Renaissance: A Study of the Fuggers and Their Connections*, trans. H. M. Lucas (New York: Harcourt, 1928); Götz von Pölnitz, *Die Fugger*, 6th ed. (Tübingen: Mohr Siebeck, 1999); Mark Häberlein, *Die Fugger: Geschichte einer Augsburger Familie (1367–1650)* (Stuttgart: Kohlhammer, 2006); ET: *The Fuggers of Augsburg: Pursuing Wealth and Honor in Renaissance Germany* (Charlottesville: University of Virginia Press, 2012). On Augsburg and monopolistic firms, see Thomas A. Brady Jr., *Turning Swiss: Cities and Empire, 1450–1550* (Cambridge: Cambridge University Press, 1985), 119–27.

Noonan writes that Eck's performance in this episode "is of great importance to the history of usury, for he made the triple contract known both to all the learned world of Europe and to the merchant bankers of his time."[62]

When Musculus' position is compared with Reformed contemporaries Martin Bucer, John Calvin, and Heinrich Bullinger, the Augsburg preacher and Bernese professor seems remarkably inflexible.[63] Perhaps his direct experiences with the Fuggers and the poorer classes in Augsburg go some way in explaining his trenchant criticisms of usury, including loans at interest to wealthy merchants. As Brady writes, "Urban antimonopoly sentiment developed as a defense of old, corporate, and collective values against the invasion of privileged wealth."[64] It would be too facile, however, to simply point to the economic power of the Fuggers, and the theological support lent to them by churchmen such as Johann Eck, to explain Wolfgang Musculus' seemingly singular rejection of usury as "damnable and most foreign to a profession of Christian justice."[65] Thus, in our sensitivity to attend to nondogmatic causes for dogmatic constructions, we must beware of downplaying the importance or denying the reality of key doctrinal interrelationships.[66]

---

62. Noonan, *The Scholastic Idea of Usury*, 209.

63. Noonan writes that "in allowing profit on loans to wealthy merchants," Calvin "permits no more than Angelus, Biel, Summenhart, Cajetan, and Eck had permitted in approving the triple contract." See Noonan, *The Scholastic Idea of Usury*, 367.

64. Brady, *Turning Swiss*, 121.

65. Musculus, *On Righteousness, Oaths, and Usury*, 91.

66. See Heiko A. Oberman, *The Two Reformations*, ed. Donald Weinstein (New Haven: Yale University Press, 2003), 65: "Only by entering into the social history of ideas, combining in thick description the mud and the marketplace, the guildhall and the council chamber, can we possibly overcome confessional triumphalism and pursue the critical task of evenhanded adjudication, considering the stake of all parties in the unavoidable clash we call Reformation." See also Muller, *After Calvin*, 44: "The point is not, of course, for intellectual history to be dissolved into social his-

Indeed, Musculus' opposition to usury is not as comprehensive as it might appear upon first glance. Musculus recognizes that the righteousness that is expected of the Christian is not the same as that which is required by the civil magistrate, and so Musculus' main concern is to address whether it is legitimate for a Christian to engage in usury. His primary focus thus is not on whether usury should be made illegal in all cases, for "civil laws do not forbid all things which are illicit before God, and, besides, those things which they do not forbid they also do not punish."[67] Musculus uses this distinction to explain why it may be acceptable in certain times and places for the civil magistrate to refrain from banning all forms of usury, even if no form of usury could ever meet the higher standard of Christian righteousness. He states quite plainly that "we are inquiring in this place about usury, whether it is lawful or unlawful, not before the world, but before God," and thus "the pretext of civil law and whatever sort of human arrangement that may exist cannot have a place in this question."[68] It is with this pastoral rather than political or civil concern in mind that Musculus also avoids the intricacies of medieval scholastic debates concerning legitimate

tory—rather, the issue is for the historian of ideas to recognize consistently that the ideas belong to a particular historical context and that the context may be defined socially or politically within a very narrow geographical or chronological frame, just as it may be defined by a particular debate that was little informed or influenced by immediate social issues."

67. Musculus, *On Righteousness, Oaths, and Usury*, 85.

68. Musculus, *On Righteousness, Oaths, and Usury*, 87. In this, Musculus' perspective is closer to that of Zwingli than to that of Bucer and Calvin, who arguably had a greater focus on questions regarding the propriety of civil laws regarding usury. Compare Ramp, *Das Zinsproblem*, 73–76. See also Baker, "Heinrich Bullinger and the Idea of Usury," 50: "If it had been possible, Zwingli would have had no *Zins*. Because that was not possible, because of the institution of private property and the sinfulness of man, he tried to ameliorate the existing situation."

interest.[69] This is not to say that Musculus ignores the patristic and medieval exegetical and legal traditions but rather that the genre of this work is not scholastic in a strict sense. We can see from his citations of standard sources in the history of exegesis and Gratian's *Decretum*, for instance, that Musculus' argument was formed in dialogue with a host of medieval antecedents.

Musculus' argument against usury progresses through differentiation between the parties involved with the usurer in the transaction. First, Musculus addresses the impropriety of lending at guaranteed profit to the poor. Next, Musculus moves on to question usurious lending to princes and merchants. Musculus concludes by examining the issue of usurious lending to widows and orphans. Each of these three classes of usury is to be rejected, although not always for precisely the same reasons.

A great deal of his discussion is spent on the question of usurious lending to the poor, which Musculus concludes is not only contrary to the justice of Christ (i.e., charity), but also to the laws of nature. Lending at profit to the poor "is not only condemned as inhuman by the laws of Christ, but also by the laws of nature. It is plainly inhuman to pursue a profit from the sweat and calamities of the poor."[70]

The entire discussion of usury is remarkably focused on the ethical implications of the practice, in harmony with Musculus'

69. Thus, Musculus writes, "To be sure, the scholastic decisions are no less complex than the intricate nature of this sort of avarice, but I will by no means touch upon that topic, but, rather, I will simply mention those things that, it seems to me, must be said without any sort of thorny debate." See Musculus, *On Righteousness, Oaths, and Usury*, 80. See also Baker, "Heinrich Bullinger and the Idea of Usury," 50: "When the Protestant reformers considered the topic of usury, they dealt mainly with the Biblical prohibitions and the sterility of money, ignoring the detailed analysis of the scholastics." For a discussion of the legitimate forms of interest allowed in the medieval era, see Noonan, *The Scholastic Analysis of Usury*, 100–132.

70. Musculus, *On Righteousness, Oaths, and Usury*, 99–100. Calvin appeals to a "common principle of justice" in making the same judgment. See Calvin, *Commentary on the Book of Psalms*, 1:213.

tropological exegetical emphasis. Musculus identifies the root of usury as avarice or greed, "the pursuit of one's own advantage," which is never an acceptable Christian purpose.[71] In this way, Musculus is more concerned about the internal motivation behind usurious practice rather than adjudicating the question of any social or external benefit. As he writes in the body text of the commentary on Psalm 15, "We must also consider not only what should be done, but in what spirit it may be done. In fact, those things which have the appearance of good can be done in such a way that they are evil, not good."[72] Musculus admits that money can be put into use to produce wealth but contends that if this is done out of avarice, then the results are morally disastrous:

> Moreover, nowhere do I find that the Lord has promised that he wishes us to preserve and nourish ourselves by usury in leisure and luxury. Therefore, rather, what it is to test the Lord is to live in leisure, to dedicate one's children also to leisure, and meanwhile to hope that the money that is annually received by usury will be able to provide perpetually so that one may be a slave not only to necessary enjoyments, but also to luxuries and delicacies.[73]

When abundance of wealth is added to someone whose focus is intemperately directed at material and temporal goods, the works of charity are obfuscated.

---

71. Musculus, *On Righteousness, Oaths, and Usury*, 100.

72. Musculus, *On Righteousness, Oaths, and Usury*, 24. Recall that Musculus' definition of usury involves the "hope" or "expectation" of gain. In focusing on the "spirit" in which things must be done to be righteous, Musculus' analysis shares features with the treatments of usury by other reformers, even though in the end Musculus disagrees that there could ever be "innocent and legitimate occasions for lending at interest." See Norman Jones, *God and the Moneylenders: Usury and Law in Early Modern England* (Cambridge, MA: Basil Blackwell, 1989), 19.

73. Musculus, *On Righteousness, Oaths, and Usury*, 101–2.

Interestingly enough, Musculus does not seem to base his arguments about the impermissibility of usury on the classical argument that money is a nonfungible and sterile measure. He acknowledges the productivity of money as it is employed in various ways, but this reality does not excuse the vice of the usurer. The Christian is called neither to lend at profit nor to lend at all but rather to lend gratuitously to those from whom the prospect of repayment is slim, to those who have never had the means to give a loan, to friends as well as enemies, and to those from whom no gratitude or thanks can be expected.[74]

Musculus' restrictive approach to usury stands in more direct continuity with the dominant medieval rejection of usury than do the approaches of many of his Reformed contemporaries. His position on usury is important, therefore, not because Musculus represents a development of the inevitable march of economic progress through history but because he shows that there was no unanimous Protestant or Reformed consensus on the question of usury in the sixteenth century.

Indeed, the disputes that had arisen in the late medieval era between distinctively permissive and restrictive attitudes toward usury do not come over into the Reformation along confessionally identifiable lines. The opinion of Petrus Canisius, the Jesuit who came to Augsburg after Musculus' departure, is a good example of this. Canisius, unlike a number of his Roman Catholic contemporaries, steadfastly opposed the validity of the triple contract.[75] As Norman Jones summarizes aptly, "The

74. Musculus, *On Righteousness, Oaths, and Usury*, 90.

75. See Klaus Hansen, "Petrus Canisius's Stand on Usury: An Example of Jesuit Tactics in the German Counter Reformation," *Archiv für Reformationsgeschichte* 55, no. 2 (1964): 192–204. Hansen argues that Canisius' opposition is due in large part to his sensitivity to the particular social and economic environment in Augsburg. This would in part explain the consistency between the attitudes of Musculus and Canisius on usury, given that both were at different times concerned to advance their particular confessional causes among the townspeople of Augsburg.

coming Reformation did little to change attitudes toward usury, and usury doctrines never became a partisan issue between Protestants and Catholics."[76] In the Reformation era, as in the later Middle Ages, there continued to be two basic positions on usury, and both sides continued to enjoy vociferous support.[77]

## Conclusion

The appendices on usury and oaths provide us with a clear contrast in exegetical result through the use of a consistent exegetical method. The injunctions of Christ against usury and oaths in the New Testament seem at first glance to be equally stringent. We are to loan without expecting anything in return just as we are not to swear by anything. However, for Musculus' exegetical process, the background provided by the broader New Testament context and the received Old Testament attitudes are determinative for his exegetical result. Where both usury and oaths are apparently rejected by Christ in the New Testament, in the Old Testament usury is prohibited while oaths are obligatory. These basic attitudes of approval toward legitimate oaths and disapproval of lending at profit are also represented in the medieval approaches to these questions.

In this psalm in particular, it is shown to be a positive mark of the righteous to swear and be true to an oath but not to lend at usury. The interpretive method employed by Musculus, which compares Christ's injunctions against oaths and usury to the broader biblical and traditional witnesses, is the same for both questions. Musculus interprets Jesus' proscriptions with this question in mind: "How is it fitting that the justice of the law of Moses is more complete than the gospel of Christ?"[78] The larger scriptural witness on the validity of oaths and usury diverges in

76. Jones, *God and the Moneylenders*, 19.

77. See especially Jones, *God and the Moneylenders*, 19.

78. Musculus, *On Righteousness, Oaths, and Usury*, 88.

the Old Testament, however, approving the former but disapproving of the latter. It is this consistent hermeneutical approach that critically determines Musculus' exegetical and doctrinal result.

Musculus' commentary on Psalm 15, including the appendices on oaths and usury, has a threefold significance. First, the commentary stands as a significant example of the application of interpretive method in the history of exegesis, as Musculus comes to two radically different conclusions about seemingly equivalent prohibitions in the words of Christ, based in part upon their respective approbation or proscription in the psalm. Second, Musculus' psalm exegesis and appendices function as topical moral texts, forerunners of later and more developed Protestant ethical thought and casuistry. Finally, Musculus' treatment of oaths and usury are representative of influential streams of Reformed thought on social, political, legal, and ethical affairs that continued to be formative for the next two centuries.

# On Righteousness, Oaths, and Usury

## A Commentary on Psalm 15

# Psalm 15*

## Argument of the Psalm

*In this psalm the prophet recites that whoever wishes to have fellowship with God and to acquire an immovable residence in both his church and kingdom, by necessity must devote himself to true and solid righteousness.*

A Psalm of David

1 O Lord, who will abide in your tabernacle? Who will dwell on your holy mountain?[1]

2 Whoever walks blamelessly, does righteousness, and speaks the truth in his heart.

3 Whoever does not slander with his tongue, whoever does not cause evil for his neighbor and does not support a reproach against his neighbor.

---

* This translation is based on Wolfgang Musculus, *In Davidis Psalterium sacrosanctum Commentarij: In quibus et reliqua catholicae religionis nostrae Capita passim, non praetermissis orthodoxorum etiam Patrum sententijs, ita tractantur, ut Christianus lector nihil desiderare amplius possit* (Basel: Herwagen, 1573), 122–32. Editorial additions are marked in the main text by brackets, and the reference apparatus contains editorial notes.

1. Throughout this work, Musculus uses the Latin term *Dominus* in place of the tetragrammaton. To convey this our translation will utilize "Lord."

4In whose eyes an abominable thing is despised, and who, while fearing, glorifies the Lord. He swears to his neighbor and does not change.
5Whoever does not give his money at usury and does not accept a bribe against the innocent. Whoever does these things will not be moved forever.

## Reading

### Verse 3

*Whoever does not slander with his tongue*. The Hebrew reads: לארגל לשונו ("Whoever does not slander"). The Greek reads: ὅς οὐκ ἐδόλωσεν ἐν γλωσσῃ ("Whoever does not distort with his tongue"). The Latin Vulgate reads: "Whoever does not deliver deceit in his speech." Jerome's Vulgate reads: "Whoever is not easy in his own speech." The Chaldee reads: "His tongue has not easily disparaged." Felix reads: "His tongue has not slandered."[2]

### Verse 4

*He swears to his neighbor.* The Hebrew reads: נשבע להרע ("He swears to his own hurt"). Jerome reads: "He swears so that he may afflict himself." The Chaldee and several more recent translations also read in this way. The rest have no discrepancy.

---

2. It is probable that Musculus is consulting a contemporary polyglot edition of the Psalms. The Felix referenced above probably refers to Felix of Prato (Felix Pratensis, d. 1539), a Jew who converted to Roman Catholicism, whose edition of the Psalms, first published in 1515, was included in *Psalterium sextuplex: Hebraeum, cum tribus Latinis, uidelicet, Diui Hieronymi, R. P. Sanctis Pagnini, & Felicis Pratensis: Graecum, Septuaginta interpretum, cum Latina uulgata* (Lyons: Sebastianus Gryphius, 1530).

## Explanation

### Verse 1

*O LORD, who will abide, etc.* It appears that David, as both prophet and king, when he brought the ark of the covenant to mount Zion and composed this psalm in that place (just as we read in 2 Samuel 6[:12–23] and 1 Chronicles 16[:8–36]), exhorts and urges the people of God to the fear of God and to a true zeal for real righteousness. David desired, if this were pleasing to God, to establish God's throne among them, in a certain place (namely on Mt. Zion). God condescended to be worshiped and adored—something they would not want to lose, something in which they should dwell conscientiously, dutifully, and justly. Thus he prophesises in this way: "O LORD, who will abide in your tabernacle?" In this verse, he employs an interrogatory apostrophe to God, not saying simply, "Who will abide in the tabernacle of God? Who will dwell on his holy mountain?" but, "O LORD, who will abide in your tabernacle? Who will dwell on your holy mountain?" so that God personally, so to speak, should respond to his question and accomplish the things that follow, and so that these words should be more reverently heard and remembered, as they were set forth not by a human spirit but by a divine oracle. Moreover, he says the same thing twice. Indeed he means the same thing by the tabernacle of God as by his holy mount. He does this to stir up the souls of the pious so that they may be admonished that they are to dwell not simply in Jerusalem but in the tabernacle and on the holy mountain of God.

## Observation

### Verse 1

First, we must consider why he honors the city of Zion, the holy tabernacle, and the mountain of God. This city was large and robust when he acquired the fortifications and city by his zeal, and also had swept away the Jebusites. In fact, he does not boast of any of this, nor does he commend to the people of the Lord the greatness and vigor of this city, but, rather, he sings about the tabernacle and holy mountain of God so that he may preach the grace of God and encourage that which must be preferred to the vigor and greatness of this city.

Next, what also must be considered is that he assigns a tabernacle and mountain for God on the earth. The Lord who fills heaven and earth does not dwell in things made by hands, yet he desired that some place for the celebration of his name should exist among his own people where his flock might be fed in the fear and worship of God, where it might hear the law of its own God, where it might be reminded of his kindnesses, where it might be established under figures and shadows, where it might be unified in one body, and separated and distinguished from the rest of all the nations of the earth. On account of this, he promised a place for his own presence over the place of the atonement on the ark. For this reason, because all things were customarily done in this place under shadows and types, in order that they would not be despised, he called it the house of God, the city of God, the dwelling place of God, the throne of God, the temple of God, the tabernacle of God, the holy mountain of God, and similar things. Indeed, just as customarily happens in the majority of cases on account of the corrupted nature of our flesh, the fleshly Jews abused those clauses thinking that they had God in a box, in a tabernacle, and in a temple. As a result they thought that it could not happen that they would be imperiled in any treaty concerning the state of their own affairs, on account of the presence of their own God, even if they should live most shamefully and should be a people without any faith, righteousness, and piety. See the history of when the ark of God was carried to the camp against the Philistines in 1 Samuel 4. For that reason, the prophets customarily cried out that God did not dwell in things made by hands. See also Acts 7 where Stephen with great confidence upbraided not simply the coarse common people but those of the first rank—the Pharisees, the scribes, the priests—and in their own council no less! Judge here what could be opposed to those who shut Christ up in a stony sanctuary, and who subscribe to this rule: "Bow the knee, in this place, O venerable stone, to Christ the host."[3] At any rate, they should hear the apostle saying in Hebrews 9[:24] that "Jesus has not entered into that which has been made by hands, which are examples of the actual things, but into heaven itself, so that he may now appear before the face of God for us." Concerning the Mount Zion of God, see the previous commentary on Psalm 2:6.

Third, it must be observed that God personally examines and speaks to those who dwell within his tabernacle and on his mountain. The prophet signifies by this examination that God magnifies his tabernacle and his holy mountain in order that it may be entirely perceived that not just anyone dwells in it, but that this grace of dwelling in it pertains to those who are deemed worthy by that grace. Additionally, the privilege of dwelling on it is denied to the unworthy and the impious. In any case, there is no reason to examine his method. Those sorts of questions are trivial and also vulgar, and no one examines these things who has mastered them. We are only examining the choice and outstanding things and are not rashly touching upon all things.

Fourth, we might also consider that the text does not say, "O Lord, who will enter your tabernacle? Who will approach your holy mountain?" but, "Who will abide in your tabernacle?" and,

---

3. This quote, "Flecte genu, lapis hic venerabilis, hospite Christo," loosely matches an epigram in letter XXXII of Paulinus of Nola, in reference to pictures and inscriptions in the basilica he designed and had built, see Migne's *Patrologia Latina* (Paris, 1847), 61:332. The exact inscription as cited by Musculus can also be found, for example, in Saint-Georges chapel at the cathedral Notre-Dame de Caudebec, see Cochet's *Les eglises de l'arrondisement d'Yvetot*, vol. 1 (Paris: Didron, 1852), 30. A slightly different version is found in Maria Kerk in Utrecht: "Flecte genu, domus haec venerabilis, hospite Christo," see K. Sprunger, *Dutch Puritanism: A History of English and Scottish Churches of the Netherlands in the Sixteenth and Seventeenth Centuries* (Leiden: Brill, 1982), 215–16.

"Who will dwell on your holy mountain?" By the words *dwelling* and *abiding* he portrays the dwelling place as immovable. The former phrasing is an occasional occurrence and the latter phrasing is such that once we have been admitted, we constantly remain and are preserved there. The latter of the two is the only true state. Let us think, for instance, about the church and the reign of Christ, to whom we are yoked, and how dear it should be to us because it has been given to us to dwell on the holy mountain of God, and so we should take care that we conduct ourselves in such a way that we would not at some point be ejected. For which of the faithful is ignorant of the fact that a zeal for piety and righteousness ought to be preeminent in us, who do not dwell in a shadowy tabernacle and mount but in the kingdom of the Son of God, and who have been transported into that truth?

## Explanation

### Verse 2

*Whoever walks blamelessly, etc.* A question quite necessarily set forward requires a perspicuous and splendid response, especially because the prophet treats the subject openly enough and covers it in a few words. Moreover, he uses an arrangement and order in such a way that he may briefly cover the whole thing first and then distribute it into parts. The chief point is this: Whoever walks blamelessly, that is, whoever lives and conducts themselves blamelessly walking in integrity, embraces the deeds and words in themselves throughout their whole life and conversation. (The distribution of this statement into its terms follows.) He says, "Whoever walks blamelessly." The Hebrew reads: הלך תמים. Moreover, תמין signifies what is whole and perfect. Thus we read in Exodus 12[:5], בן שנה שה תמים זכר, that is, a "blameless, one-year-old male lamb." Moreover it is called a blameless lamb "without any defect" (Lev. 22[:19–21]). The majority of the interpreters of the Holy Scriptures render *blameless* as *simplicity*—a translation that rightly squares with the expression תמים, if it is understood correctly, of course, that simple is the same thing as bright, blameless, and harmless. Its opposite is slyness, cleverness, and the duplicity of a perverse heart. In that sense, the passage ought to be understood as: "He who walks simply, walks well." Whoever abhors the knowledge of the Holy Scriptures abuses this expression, as if to walk simply is to walk ignorantly without any knowledge of the divine truth and true piety.

*And he accomplishes righteousness and speaks the truth in his own heart.* In these words that he spoke, "whoever walks blamelessly," he divides the matter by a brief distribution into words and deeds. For by deeds and words the behavior of our whole life is evident. Moreover, it is to accomplish righteousness and to strive for righteousness and uprightness. For here is set forth צדק or "righteousness" (which we Germans call *Frombkeit* and the Latins call *probitas*, for which reason they are called good men). He "speaks the truth," it says, "in his own heart." Here is the other part of the distribution concerning the righteousness of words. To speak the truth from the heart is nothing other than to speak in good faith as well as candidly and sincerely from the heart, which is to speak the truth. Its opposite is to speak deceitfully and maliciously something other than the truth and also to hide something other than the truth in one's heart, concerning which we have seen the same point previously made in my commentary on Psalm 12. He complains that a craftiness and maliciousness of heart and of speech prevailed everywhere among mortals in his own time.

## Observation

### Verse 2

*Whoever walks blamelessly.* In this passage, the chief point that must be observed is that kind of righteousness that the prophet prescribes to those who would remain inhabitants of the tabernacle and holy mountain of God. He clearly requires that sort of righteousness from those people that does not exist in the ceremonies and legal shadows only, but that embraces the whole life and also lives and breathes true honesty of soul and charity toward one's neighbor. He understood that it is the character of the flesh to think first of commending oneself only to God without any indwelling reckoning of one's neighbor. Next, that sort of person only studies the righteousness that is situated in the external ceremonies and ecclesiastical rites, and that may be exercised in temples and shrines. Among the Jews, inasmuch as there was circumcision, the sacrificing of sheep, not eating various things, washing in water by purging the body but not the spirit, and whatever other things pertaining to the Jewish rites, they were measuring true piety and righteousness before God in those sorts of things. We see in the Scriptures that the prophets wrestled against such superstitions. Therefore, it does not say, "whoever might be circumcised, whoever might offer sheep in the tabernacle or in the temple, whoever might wash frequently, whoever might not touch something polluted," but rather, "whoever walks blamelessly, does righteousness, and speaks the truth in his heart," and so forth. He certainly does not reject those things that the law commanded pertaining to ceremonial things. Indeed, on the contrary, he summons the people of God from that opinion and Jewish superstition by which they pledge themselves before God to true piety and righteousness by the observing of the ceremonies; and he exhorts them to a zeal for real righteousness, showing that a whole and just life is required by God (Isa. 1[:16–19]; Jer. 7[:1–7]; Ps. 40[:3–11]; 50[:14, 23]; 51[:16–17]).

What will we say here concerning the superstition of the pseudo-Christians who think that they worship and please God apart from a renovation of life and a zeal for true righteousness, having sought it from ceremonies and not from the word of God, but in fact from human contrivances? Let the impious persons roar in the Gentile temples more than in the Christian ones. If you examine their life—the carnal, the impudent, the fornicators, the simoniacs, the idolaters, and the like—they think that this roaring of theirs, together with the rest of their hypocrisy and playacted scenes, is the worship of God. Indeed, they do not believe that the uneducated, common people can think. They persuade themselves of this so that they may hunt for the basest profit and look out for their own leisure and belly.

Next, it must be examined that he says, "whoever walks in integrity." If you seek briefly how the prophet requires this from a citizen of the kingdom of God, it is an easy case to prove that God delights in integrity of life and is averse to malice and fraudulence. Thus, in Proverbs 11[:20] it says that "the extravagant in heart are an abomination to the LORD, and those who walk in integrity are well-pleasing to him." He spoke to Abraham in this way: "Walk before me and be blameless" [Gen. 17:1]. Moses says to the people of God, "You will be blameless before the LORD your God" (Deut. 18[:3]). Thus men are declared תמימים that is, "blameless," such as Jacob, Job, and the rest.

In short, the phrase "whoever walks blamelessly" includes all things in itself, whether they are things that must be done for God or for human beings. Each person should apply this rule to his own situation. If you are a minister of the word, see that you enjoy that gift blamelessly, not only teaching those things that are true, but also with a blameless heart toward God and human beings, regarding neither your own glory nor your own convenience but rather the glory of God and the salvation of mortals. The same is true if you have been established as a magistrate, take heed that you judge justly and act with a blameless heart. In such a manner, this must be pondered concerning every particular thing. I speak concerning those who are God's. In that state that is against God, no one can walk blamelessly.

*And does righteousness and speaks the truth in his heart.* Here it must be noted that he divides the word *walking*—through which metaphor he expresses the whole conduct of our life—into deeds and words. "And," he says, "does justice and speaks the truth in his heart." Therefore, we are admonished to express our mind in integrity both in words and deeds so that we may not do or say anything that is malicious or unjust. It also must be observed how the word *walking* is divided into deeds and words and how he divides the expression *blamelessness* into righteousness and truth. He classifies it as righteousness in deeds and truth in speech. Therefore, righteousness is the blamelessness of our works and truth is the blamelessness of our words, and also because righteousness is in the deeds so also truth is in the words. Third, he does not say, "and knows righteousness," but "and does righteousness." It is easily learned what is right, what is not right, what ought to be done, and what ought not to be done. A true zeal for righteousness is not found in a bare knowledge alone, but is located in its practice. We do not reject knowledge, but we require the sort that is living and effective. For a pious person, to know righteousness is not simply to know what it is, but to press it out into one's deeds. Moreover, righteousness must be done in such a way that what is one's due may be rendered chiefly and for each person. In general, let us owe nothing to anyone except that we should love one another (Rom. 13[:8]). Not only does the law (*instrumentum*) of the Old Testament require it, but also the law (*lex*) of the New Testament requires it.[4] Next, it is noted what pastors and teachers of Christ's church owe; what, in turn, believers owe to their own pastors and teachers; what a magistrate owes to his subjects; what subjects owe to their magistrates; what husbands owe to their wives; what parents owe to their children; what children owe to their parents; what a master owes to his servant; what a servant owes to his master; what citizens owe to other citizens; what neighbors owe to their neighbors, and so forth. Let each person consider in what way he may accomplish righteousness: first, toward persons in general; second, toward those to whom he is especially connected.

4. In this instance, Musculus uses *instrumentum* in the legal sense of a deed, will, or contract, just as modern English might speak of a will as a legal instrument.

*And he speaks the truth in his own heart.*

*And he speaks.* This clause has been placed here for a singular reason. Indeed, I do not say a large part, but, in actuality, the greatest and most noteworthy part of human life includes the use of speech. From whom it is taken away, what is their life but like some kind of speechless story enveloped in the darkness of errors? The gift of speaking is an utterly excellent thing. Among all living things, it is granted as a divine gift only to humans, from which point also scholars judged that this is proper to a person, and they defined a person as a bipedal animal that knows how to speak. The use of speaking truly extends broadly. Indeed, it can be confined to these terms: first to serve the glory of God, second for human uses. It serves the glory of God in the praising of his name and in the preaching of the truth and grace of his kingdom. It serves human association, first, in order to reveal the necessary deliberations of our hearts in words, by which things we indicate what is necessary for us, whatever we may want, whatever we may seek, command, desire, and ask. Next, it serves human association so that we may also look out for the advantages and the needs of our neighbors. It may happen that either we will teach the ignorant and lead back the erring into the way, or rebuke the delinquent, or praise those doing well, or pacify the enraged, or console and encourage the sorrowful, and by speaking we procure whatever other necessity that our neighbor requires. This preeminent gift of God, necessary on so many accounts, without which no one knows what is in a person, is corrupted partly from the fickleness of the human heart and partly from the heart's malice and fraud, so that it is not contrary to reason that this is included as part of doing righteousness. Therefore, we are reminded that those who desire to be citizens of the kingdom of God ought to consider not only what is required of them in this way so that they may have a rationale for their own deeds, but also so that in their words they may be found blameless and irreproachable.

*The truth.* First, we should consider that he does not say, "and he speaks loosely, ingeniously, wisely, elegantly, ornately, and magnificently," but "and he speaks the truth." Therefore the truth is that which is required in someone's words who desires to be a citizen of the kingdom of God, in whatever way the truth is brought forward in words, whether many or few, whether simple or ornate and elegant, so that it may not happen that some rude and uneducated person who is ignorant of language is excused. This is the nature and condition of the truth that someone may rejoice in its simple perspicuity, even as it is honorably dressed just like a chaste matron. The truth lacks the cosmetics and complexion of lies that are comparable to a brazen and lascivious harlot. Therefore, whoever requires a laborious study of elegance in regard to the truth is excessively self-indulgent and equally appears to act like some husband who entreated his wife to mimic the lascivious and shameful way that harlots dress, for which reason men seem to delight in harlots. Next, let us also consider why the Holy Spirit requires truth in the speech of the citizens of the kingdom of God. First, because truth is a certain kind of divine thing, and God who is so truthful that he does not know how to deceive, delights in the utmost in the truth and detests a lie as the invention of the devil and contrary to the truth. Next, because the use of speech (which we cannot do without) depends on the truth and is perverted and corrupted when it is severed from the truth, just as if you deprived the sun of its splendor, the earth of its fertility, water of its wetness, stones of their hardness, and fire of its heat. For just as each of God's creatures has been given something so that the utility of that creature is evident, likewise that something is necessary to be present in each human work, by which the work is what it is. It is evident, whether you may call it right or whole in general, that without that something the utility of those things cannot exist. It is just as if the foundation of a house is not firm and the foundation does not rest in a settled way, so that the foundation cannot sustain the mass of the shrines built upon it, or, likewise, if the roof may not be duly fit together with tiles, or if the beams and walls are not rightly assembled and covered, or if a sword is not sharpened, but dull, not hardened, but malleable.[5] Thus also is the condition of human speech, which depends on the truth, so that without it not only is it useless, but it is also rather harmful, so that it is not without reason that truth is required from the pious. Third, it should not be ignored that it does not say, "and speaks the whole truth," but simply, "and speaks the truth." It is not required from a citizen of the kingdom of God that he should speak the whole truth, that is, whatever is true. First, for instance, it is not the case that any one person knows the whole truth, but only God does. Moreover, how could anyone speak the truth that is unknown to him? Nor is it evident that we should utter immediately whatever we know is true. Furthermore, it must also appear to a good man that he should either declare the truth or remain silent in such a way as he judges it profitable for his neighbor. As a matter of fact, it is not the truth of our speech, but charity, which is our whole rule and goal, not only in the things that we do, but also in the things we say. That is why even holy men at times concealed the truth sometimes by being silent and other times by speaking. Like Joseph, when he was falsely accused by the wife of his master Potiphar, he preferred to bear the injury patiently rather than reveal the crime of his mistress by speaking the truth (Gen. 39[:1–19]). The Egyptian midwives did not sin when they did not reveal to the tyrannical Pharaoh the truth that they certainly knew about the Hebrew women, but rather sheltered them with some kind of fabrication (Ex. 1[:15–21]). Michal (1 Sam. 19[:11–17]) and Jonathan (1 Sam. 20:[5–34]) did not commit a sin when they did not reveal the truth concerning David to the impious Saul, although he was their father. Indeed, there are so many sorts of these things in the Scriptures concerning this question of

5. *plumbeus*: lit. "leadened." The contrast is between a sword comprised of hardened and tempered steel versus malleable and brittle lead.

whether it is permissible for a good man sometimes to say what is not true; and concerning a lie, see our commentary on John 8[:44], where it says, "because he is a liar, and the father of such."

*In his own heart.* We observe here that he does not simply say, "and speaks the truth," but he adds, "in his own heart." First, it can happen that someone may speak falsely what he yet thinks in his own heart is true. On the other hand, it can happen that he may speak the truth with his mouth while he yet thinks in his heart that it is false. Thus he says rightly, "and he speaks the truth in his own heart." He does not say, "in his neighbor's heart," but "in his own heart." He is innocent who says what he says because he thinks in his own heart that it is true, even if it may be false in the hearts of others, if only he does not act against the rule of charity. He is false who speaks the truth with his mouth while he thinks in his own heart that it is not true.

Next, it could happen that what is true, and what he knows to be true, he speaks from the mouth only and not from the heart, just as it also happens on the contrary that what is false, and what he knows to be false, he mentions with his mouth only and not from the heart. That which happens for good comes to pass sometimes out of fear. It is like what happened to Peter when he said, "I have not known the man," because it was false, and he was speaking with his mouth and not from the heart [Luke 22:57–60; John 18:15–17]. Likewise, in this passage it is required from one who ought to be a citizen of the kingdom of God that he speak not only from his mouth, but also from his heart what he knows or thinks is true so that he is a person who not only speaks true things, but also is a lover of and devotee to the truth and is such a person not only toward God, but also toward his neighbor. As a matter of fact, as it concerns God, what sort of person is able to deceive God? On the contrary, who else but God is present for the use of our words and who intimately knows all the secrets of our hearts, even if we are entirely mute?

## Observation

### Verse 3

*Whoever does not slander with his tongue, etc.* The prophet, not content with a summary of the righteousness of words and deeds, descends to examine certain kinds of righteousness, which we will inspect in order. Among all the vices of the tongue that are innumerable, he sets forth the worst two: slander, of course, and perjury, of which he will make mention in the following verse. He rejects slander in the first place because it has a rather broad domain, and also it is much less recognized how much sin it encompasses. The Hebrew is לארגל, which word means "to spy." From which מרגלים are called spies. Therefore, the prophet shows that he rejects the worst kinds of persons that thoroughly search for the secrets of a neighbor with flattering and fictitious words and, in the manner of a spy, convey something else with their tongues.

*Nor does he cause evil for his neighbor.* This pertains to the righteousness of deeds and to an innocence of life. It is the character of a righteous and innocent person not to wound his neighbor in any matter either by his words or deeds, but rather to conduct himself in such a way toward anyone with an eagerness for charity so that he may desire not to trouble anyone knowingly. Thus, this clause, in which he says, "nor does he cause evil for his neighbor," must be understood so that to cause evil for his neighbor is the same thing as to trouble his neighbor knowingly and willingly.

*And he does not support a charge against his neighbor.* This passage is variously exposited on account of the Hebrew expression נשא, which sometimes means "to accept," other times "to carry," and also quite frequently "to suffer." Some exposit this phrase, "and he does not lay a charge against his neighbor," as meaning that he will not denigrate the reputation and name of his neighbor. Others exposit this phrase, "and he does not report a charge against his neighbor"—that is, he does not commit something that his neighbor can change into a charge against him. Others exposit it (just as we translated it here) so that it should be understood that it is not appropriate for a righteous man to lay a charge against his own neighbor—that is, to allow some mark of ignominy to be branded upon his neighbor in his presence. The Holy Spirit expels such a disposition from a citizen of the kingdom of God so that he neither personally slanders his neighbor nor suffers that it may be done in his presence by anyone, but, on the contrary, he defends his neighbor's name with that zeal with which he desires his own name to be defended.

*Whoever does not slander with his tongue.* So that we may estimate the vice of slander as exceedingly detestable, these points must be considered: (1) what it is, (2) what is its origin, (3) what is its quality, (4) what are its circumstances, and (5) how it is harmful.

### 1. What It Is to Slander One's Neighbor

To slander one's neighbor is not simply to report what the neighbor either says or does (because sometimes not only is this permissible to do, but also it ought to be done either for their sake or for the public good), but it is to report something maliciously, in the spirit of harming one's neighbor. For this reason also the prophet used the word רגל. Those who showed to the chief priest Eli the wickedness of his sons were not slanderers, concerning which he said, "It is an evil which I hear about you, my sons" (1 Sam. 2[:23]). Joseph was not a slanderer when he accused his brothers before his father about the worst crime (Gen. 37[:2]). They were not slanderers who had written to Paul about the contentions and harlotries of the Corinthians (1 Cor. 1[:5]). Doeg, who denounced David and Ahimelech before Saul, was a slanderer (1 Sam. 22[:9–10]). Those who said to Saul, "David seeks evil against you," were slanderers (1 Sam. 24[:9]).

### 2. Where Slander Takes Its Origin

A consideration of the origin of slander accomplishes the most toward renouncing this vice. It does not exist from any other place than from Satan, who in the beginning even immediately slandered Eve in her presence, saying, "By no means will you die, but God knows that in whatever day you should eat of the tree, your eyes will be opened by it, and you will be as gods, knowing good and evil" (Gen. 3[:4–5]). Again, he slandered the sons of God before God, just as is well known in the history of Job, when it is written in chapter one that he said to God, "Surely it cannot be that Job fears God for nothing? Haven't you personally fortified him by surrounding his house and all his wealth? You have blessed the works of his hands and his possessions have increased upon the earth. But extend your hand just a little, and touch all that he possesses, and he will have only appeared to have blessed you" [Job 1:9–11]. All of which was nothing other than saying, "Job does not worship you with a sincere soul, but only on account of his own particular benefits. Touch his possessions and you will see whether or not he has blessed you up to now only in appearance." On account of this malice of denouncing, Satan has this name in the Scriptures in which he is called the devil, that is, the denouncer and accuser (see Rev. 12[:9]). In the same way, therefore, he lies against those who are subject to himself, and thus he slanders them too, even disturbing that wicked concord of those brothers!

### 3. What Sort of Vice Slander Is

1. For the most part, a denouncer is a liar. As a matter of fact, he either reports something false, inventing what neither has been said nor done, or if he reports something true, he reports some things that could favor someone by its reporting, and he adds something of his own that would not favor the same person. By that addition he constructs a calumny serious in its appearance and resembling the truth, or he perverts the sense of the person's words and the reasons for their actions. In this way, Haman was inventing things against the Jews in the presence of Ahasuerus that were not true and, at the same time, stating what was true,

contaminating it so as to cause hatred. "There is a people," he was saying, "that are dispersed throughout all the provinces of your kingdom, and are distinct from you both by using strange laws and ceremonies as well as additionally despising the decrees of the king. And you know best what is not expedient for your kingdom so that they may not grow proud through license. If it pleases you, decree that they should perish" [Esther 3:8–9]. Thus, Ziba the servant of his lord Mephibosheth reported falsely to David, inventing what was not true (2 Sam. 16[:1–4]).

2. A denouncer is malicious and unjust. For he reports not simply what good things there are in his neighbor and what could be profitable to his neighbor, but also those things that are bad and that are not for his neighbor's correction but for his detriment. His eye is malicious, not observing those things that are good but only those that are evil. His ears are malicious, hearing only bad things and deaf to the good things. His speech is malicious, reporting only the bad things and being silent about the good things. These things are the nature of a denouncer.

3. He is also a counterfeit and a hypocrite, for he feigns either benevolence or good faith toward the one to whom he denounces his neighbor, or he feigns zeal for either justice or piety. Meanwhile, he excuses himself because he does not wish ill in denouncing.

4. He is also a secret ambusher, murdering in secret like a serpent so that whoever is denounced may not know who is denouncing him, and related to this point, he requires the confidence of silence in order that he may not be revealed.

### *4. The Circumstances Aggravating This Vice*

1. For the most part, it matters who the denouncer is—whether a friend, a member of a household, a brother, a subordinate, a student, a servant. At any rate, such a person sins more than if he were to denounce an acquaintance for no reason.

2. It matters whom you denounce. If it is a public person, you sin more than if it were a private person. If it is a whole family,

state, or region, you sin more immensely than if you denounce only one person.

3. The sin is increased if you slander a spouse, a master, a magistrate, a prince, a friend, a brother, or a foreigner, for in this case there is more detriment to the one denounced.

4. It also matters by which route you denounce a neighbor concerning a matter—namely, by involving either the neighbor's goods, or reputation, or friendship, or life.

5. It must also be considered in what frame of mind you might denounce someone. There are those who denounce out of a certain habit and thoughtlessness, not weighing beforehand what they say, and what disadvantage could occur to the one they have denounced. Those sorts of people seem to sin more mildly, although they cannot be excused. Let those sorts of people consider how they are corrupted and perverse in this case because they are not to the same degree inclined to report those things that are good as well as those things that are bad. Others rail against their neighbor with an eagerness to gratify the one to whom they are reporting. These commit a greater sin. Still others denounce their neighbor to pursue their own certain advantage, for example, just as Ziba, the servant of Mephibosheth, did. They are the worst kind, who machinate destruction for their neighbor by slandering him even if they could hope for no advantage from it.

### *5. How Harmful It Is*

First, charity is wounded in the one who denounces. The norm of charity is that what you do not wish to be done to you is not to be done to others. By this wounding of charity this vice gains an evil conscience for the denouncer against the one who he has denounced.

Next, charity is wounded in him to whom the neighbor is denounced. Charity is thinking well of our neighbor, not the suspicion of anything evil concerning him. Through a denunciation charity is damaged.

Third, charity is undermined in the one who has been denounced. When someone senses that he has been denounced, he is affected partly by his own sinister suspicions, partly he understands that his friendship declines with the one to whom he has been denounced, and he studiously takes precaution regarding all the things of that one to whom he has been denounced. In summary, no evil is equally harmful and insidious to Christian and brotherly charity, and so this vice of denunciation is most detestable. Regarding this matter, I pass over the fact that it lies in ambush of the lives of good men in such a way that it may justly be compared to a sword and to glowing coals.

## Observation

*He does not cause evil for his own neighbor.* The principal thing that must be considered is what evil is. The Manichees dispute the origins of evil. We judge it more preferable to consider what it is than from where it originates. There is nothing evil of all those things that are made by God, which, as the Holy Scriptures hold, have been made very well. Evil is whatever is deprived of some good and is not beneficial to our neighbor, whether it is inflicted upon his goods, or his name, or his body, or his soul. Yet, in this passage we must consider in what frame of mind you may inflict damage to your neighbor. That is to say, you may harm your neighbor in rather trivial things, as well as in rather important things, if it is for his benefit—that kind of harm is not foreign to the pious, but it is also not foreign to God. Thus, true charity inclines toward a zeal for kindness so that, if it cannot be done otherwise, it may be beneficial to harm. Again, if with an inimical mind, someone troubles his neighbor, even if it is beneficial for that person, yet it must be said that in no less way it was badly done to his neighbor, because what he did, he did not do from an eagerness for beneficence but from malfeasance. Inasmuch as anyone afflicts Christians by the loss of corporeal things, even up to that point they do not hurt them, but they are actually exceedingly useful to them. In fact, for the beloved, God works all things for good [Rom. 8:28]. Actually those who afflict Christians are evildoers, not well-doers, even though what they do from an eagerness for harming, by divine providence is rendered harmless—indeed, more correctly, advantageous and useful. The same thing must also be perceived concerning those who use the appearance of kindness for harming, whether they do it by flattering, by eating and drinking, or by presenting monetary gifts. Therefore, it is evil because it harms their neighbor, or if it does not harm, yet it is inflicted in order to harm the soul. On the other hand, it is not evil that although it seems to harm, yet it neither harms nor is intended to harm the soul, but rather is discharged with a zeal for well-doing and from a place of kindness, or is at least directed at this point so that a place can be made for true kindnesses. A parent, when chastening a son with a rod of discipline, is not doing evil. A teacher, when he instructs a student with a whipping, does not do evil. A magistrate, when he beats criminals, does not do evil. A surgeon, when he cauterizes and cuts, indeed even more when he amputates whole limbs of a wounded body, does not do evil.

Next, the degrees of eagerness for doing evil to a neighbor also must be considered. The first degree is to render evil for evil. The world excuses even this kind of evildoing—like to like, as they say. Likewise, force is permitted to repel force. Indeed, we who follow Christ have been constituted differently than this. Concerning our constitution see Matthew 5[:38–39], in which place it says, "You have heard that it was said, 'eye for an eye, tooth for a tooth.' However, I say to you, do not wish to resist evil. But if anyone should strike you on your right cheek, offer to him also the other." Furthermore, Romans 12[:17] says, "Render to no one evil for evil." The second degree of evildoing is also to do evil to the undeserving and the guiltless either out of hatred or hope of profit. This kind of malice is also worse than the previous one, and is condemned not only by Christians, but also by the world. The third degree is also the highest—not only to do evil wrongly to the deserving, next also to the guiltless, but also to those deserving good, and to render evil for good. Anyone at every point up to such a degree is evil, so that it may not be doubted that the one who does evil to his own benefactors actually will not refrain from any kind of malice, because he has reached the perfection of malice. For this reason, at this very point a citizen of the kingdom of God must strive against this disposition, so that he would not even wrong an enemy as well as one who may deserve it. If someone should have studiously shunned this degree of malice that is inferior, he will also not ascend to the middle one or all the way to the highest one, and in this way he will also not desire to be troublesome to the undeserving, still less to the well-deserving. This is what is considered by Christ whose aim it is to make his own people strangers to every pursuit of malice.

Third, because an eagerness for full piety and Christian righteousness is not perfected in our not doing what is evil, but also requires the perfection of beneficence in such a way that whoever does not do well to his neighbor when he is able is reckoned as having done evil, just as we expressly see in Matthew 5[:38–48], and as we are allowed to see in the feasting rich man [Luke 16:19–31] and in those who do not feed Christ (Matt. 25[:31–46]). It must also be considered what good is and, then, what the degrees of beneficence are.

Good is what is contrary to evil, what clearly results in an advantage to our neighbor. We must also consider not only what should be done, but in what spirit it may be done. In fact, those things that have the appearance of good can be done in such a way that they are evil, not good. On the other hand, those things that you may think are evil, may in fact be reckoned more truly good than evil. Those things that Scripture teaches concerning good works must be understood as concerning those things that are devoted to the needs and advantages of our neighbors through a devotion to well-doing by a spirit of charity. Thus, Christ says in Matthew 5[:16], “Let your light so shine before men that they should see your good works and would glorify your father who is in heaven." Here "good works" cannot refer to ecclesiastical ceremonies, which can be done by evil men and ridiculed by them also, nor are they such things in which can be observed the spirit of our fathers and can be glorified by the world. Also, the Latins call something good that is useful and practical. Thus the apostle says in Galatians [6:10], "and so while we have time, we should do good towards all, especially towards the household of faith," and in 1 Timothy [6:17–18], "Teach the wealthy in this world that they should do good, and that their riches should be in good deeds, they should be ready to give, freely sharing," and so forth. The papacy misappropriates good works to the cult of the dead saints, to images, to the buying of masses of simoniacs, papal indulgences, and the fattening of the most impure fornicators and hypocrites, and so forth. True beneficence consists in a spirit of charity and expresses the paternal goodness of God on his children. For which reason no one could be eager for good works unless he previously is good. Thus Christ says in Matthew 12[:33], "Either make the tree good, and its fruit good," and so forth.

Moreover there are also three degrees of beneficence. The first is to do well to the well-deserving. This degree pertains to an owed gratitude. It is indeed the lesser degree—of such a kind that even to an unbeliever it is wicked that someone should not repay a well-deserving person their remuneration. The second degree is to do well to those to whom you are not called to show any beneficence and who are not the kind from whom you could hope for any sort of recompense and benefit. Concerning this degree of beneficence, see Luke 14[:12–14]. The third degree is to do well even to the undeserving and to enemies. This position is the pinnacle of full and complete beneficence (concerning which, see Matthew 5[:43–47] and Romans 12[:9–21]), and so this place directs Christians to an eagerness of doing well because if someone should obtain this highest degree, we would never do evil to the undeserving, still less to a friend and to the well-deserving.

Fourth, let us also weigh that he says, "to his own neighbor," and let us also consider whom he calls our neighbor. A neighbor is someone who is bound to us at some point, either by religion, humanity, blood, affinity, friendship, either in familiar or civil society; or by proximity, or conjoined to us by some plight of necessity. God has mutually joined us together in many degrees so that there are also many occasions for this hand of love and beneficence. In Christ, a neighbor is anyone who is a Christian; in humanity, anyone who is a human, a precious person and our blood; in blood, children and the rest of our kinsmen, brothers, sisters, and the rest. The Holy Spirit employs this expression of neighbor for this reason: that he might declare what sort of neighbor we should be. For this is the proper character of a neighbor—so that what sort one should be, he would declare in this—that he is conjoined more closely to us by some circumstance. It is the nature of fire to burn, light to shine, and so forth. In the end, those who experience the force and nature of fire and light more accurately are those who draw closer to them. In this way, and according to our experience, it is more thoroughly grasped who are joined closer to us by some circumstance. Whoever upholds no evil against his neighbor declares adequately that he is not devoted to an eagerness for malice. On the other hand, whoever does well to his neighbor as his neighbor, whoever that may be, clearly renders concerning himself an adequate proof of his goodness. It is easy not to harm someone who is distant from oneself, but not to cause any difficulty for our neighbors in any matter, that does not exist except among the pious and the good. This matter is extensive, but at the present time my treatment suffices to scratch the surface.

## Observation

*And he does not support a reproach against his neighbor.* Here we must think about the reasons why the Spirit requires from a citizen of the kingdom of God not only that he should not slander his neighbor, but also that he watch lest he permit his neighbor to be afflicted or wounded by any abuse. The first reason for this is charity, for we ought to love our neighbors in such a way that not only do we desire not to injure them in any matter, but also that we cannot bear it patiently when it is done to them by others. A true and sincere love of neighbor entirely causes this disposition that we find in those who are affected by a singular love toward not just a few persons. We read in 1 Samuel 19 and 20 that in such a way Jonathan zealously defended the reputation and innocence of David even against his own father. The second reason is born out of equity—that is, what someone does not want done to himself he does not do to others. Conversely, those things that he requires from others toward himself, he also personally renders to others (Matt. 7[:12]). Therefore, when we have been animated in such a way that we desire that our reputation and innocence should be defended by our neighbor against the dishonesty of accusers, it is most entirely fair that we render the same thing in turn to our neighbor.

The third reason is from the necessity of blunting the malice of denouncers who join together to pluck out by the roots the kingdom of God from the people. For just as this evil is cherished by those who are delighted by denouncers (for it is quite customary in the halls of princes), so also those who detest the slandering tongue suppress and extinguish it, and they also censure and repress the slander itself. In fact, no one will easily attempt to sully the reputation of his neighbor among those whom he believes it would vehemently displease. I will also insert a fourth reason that is brought out from this: that it is fitting that citizens of the kingdom of God have and be moved by a mutual honor among themselves. Therefore, a pious person cannot bear that those who are the people of God and attached to the citizens of the kingdom of heaven should be afflicted by an abuse. That saying of the apostle is noteworthy: "surpassing one another in honor" (Romans 12[:10]).

Concerning these cases, a Christian person must take an interest in them so that he may oppose the speech of denouncers immediately and in great earnest. If a matter is in view—indeed, if someone should disparage something that is at least apparently good—then you may say, "But now you could interpret this deed of my neighbor good naturedly and well, as it is fitting for a good man to do." If what is reported is absurd and entirely wicked then you either know that it is false or uncertain or true. If you know that it is false, you should protect the innocence of your neighbor with great steadfastness, affirming that what the denouncer says has been done has in fact not been done. If it is uncertain, you should admonish the denouncer that charity does not easily believe evil concerning one's neighbor. (How corrupt is human nature that evil things concerning one's neighbor are more quickly suspected than good things! How frequently the innocence of a neighbor is wounded by an injury and a lie! How difficult it is to clear oneself of just one blemish of defamation stamped upon you by a lying neighbor!) If you know that what is reported is true, you should consider first whether it is a secret matter or a plainly evident one. If it is a secret matter, you should admonish the denouncer, so that just as at a banquet a meal covered by some skin is not disclosed, and as a guest one knows that he may by no means burst its belly for the host, then likewise just as a brother's offense is kept to himself, he should rather go and correct his brother's delinquency in secret. If you know that the offense is plainly evident, it will be either trivial or tolerable or great. If it is a trivial one or a tolerable one, you should say that it is a lapse and mistake, the sort that happens to someone daily just as if those sleeping should have a dream. There are none among mortal human beings who are entirely devoid of sin. Blessed is the one who is only guilty of these least sorts of sins! If it is great, but it happened reluctantly, contrary to his mind's intention, then excusing it is most agreeable. However, if it happened willingly, either it will be recent and rare, and it can be extenuated by the examples of the saints, and by the infirmity of our flesh, and the fear of God can be commended to him, by which all this time he should be restrained, so that he might not go to ruin speedily or often into this sin; or, it will be oft-repeated and habitual, in which case you should say that it is your neighbor's great temptation and also that it is attached to the great infirmity of his flesh. Finally, if the one who slanders your neighbor should be your neighbor's enemy, it will be most easy to say, "Would anyone actually believe that you are speaking out of a zeal for righteousness, or rather out of hatred?" If he is indeed a friend of your neighbor, or an acquaintance, a domestic, a relative, or an acquaintance conjoined by any reason at all, again you should promptly admonish him concerning how shamelessly he is behaving in slandering his neighbor to whom he is peculiarly conjoined. In sum, charity should be present, and never should be absent because it should answer back to the denouncer and show him what is required here by a citizen of God's kingdom.

Besides all this, it must also be considered that he says, "against his own neighbor." If it must not be endured by the pious that one's neighbor, whoever he may be, whether poor or rich, should be affected by some ignominy, then how much less should it be endured if it should be committed against the word of the gospel of God and of his ministers. For such kinds of abuses, by extension, are against God himself. A zeal for piety has its own order and certain degrees also. Whoever cannot endure that the estimation of a person should be polluted if he keeps this spirit out of true charity, certainly how much less could he endure that the truth of the word of God should be defamed by the slanders of impious persons. From this very cause is the beginning of our destruction because Eve deigned to hear the serpent slandering the word and precept of God, which she would not have done if she had been furnished with a zeal for God. It should be mourned over much more than merely recounted what in this regard is lacking today in many, who yet only wish to appear to be nourished by the truth.

## Explanation

### Verse 4

*In whose eyes an abominable thing is despised, and who, while fearing, glorifies the Lord. He swears to his neighbor, and does not change.* Some of the Jews, whom certain of our theologians follow, expound the previous part of this verse in the following way: In whose eyes an abominable thing is despised—that is, in their very selves, in their own eyes—likewise, as if it is rejected, it displeases a citizen of heaven. For it is allowed that he fears God and also may be zealous for piety and righteousness, yet in his very heart he judges that he is an unprofitable servant. The opinion of others seems to me to be more resembling the truth, who understand it simply that these words should be examined by a citizen of the kingdom of heaven so that he would despise reprobate, abominable, and impious persons. Conversely, if he becomes acquainted with those who fear God, he should consider their worth. He realizes that the reprobate or also the abominable are those who constantly pursue a method of living separate from the righteous and the citizens of the kingdom of God—that is, they are the sort who walk perversely, doing iniquity, speaking lies in their own heart, slandering with their tongue, doing evil to their neighbor, sustaining a reproach against their neighbor, condemning those who fear God, making much of the wicked, swearing to their neighbor and changing, giving his own money for usury, and accepting bribes against the innocent (if anyone should give one). Those who are like this are reprobate. The pious recoil from such as these. On the other hand, those who fear the Lord are those who walk blamelessly, do justice, speak the truth in their heart, do not slander with their tongue, and do not do evil to their neighbor. Those who live in such a way declare that they restrain themselves from evil in the fear of God. Regarding that phrase, "he swears to his neighbor and does not change," I have mentioned above in the reading that certain theologians read it, "he swears to his own ruin," which reading can be explained in two parts. In the first part, it can be understood regarding those legal afflictions by which the Jews used to afflict their own souls in their fast days and in other such observations (see Isaiah 58[:2–5]). They were accustomed to bind their own souls to certain afflictions by an oath (Num. 30[:1–16]). The impious used to alter oaths of this sort when they had recovered their health and also when they were overwhelmed in tribulation. Therefore, it is understood in this sense by the pious, that if someone should vow to the affliction of his own soul, he should not change what he vowed. Next, as it is understood in this way, someone vows to his own affliction and does not change. That is, even if it brings certain affliction when one has taken the oath, yet the pious will not change because they vowed, but they will faithfully keep it even when it is to their own ruin. Indeed, it is a simpler reading and supports the argument and spirit of the psalm more, so that we read: "he swears to his neighbor and does not change." The prophet spurs on this righteousness, which is declared toward his neighbor, just as is apparent to anyone who reads this psalm attentively.

## Observation

### Verse 4

*In whose eyes an abominable thing is despised.* First, observe that he calls those who are undertaking a separate way of living from the citizens of the kingdom of heaven נמאסים, that is, "reprobate" and "abominable." To be reprobate is the same thing as to be degenerate and rejected. Thus Psalm 118[:22] says, יאבן מאסו הבונים, that is, "and the stone which the builders rejected." Jeremiah 6[:30] says, כסח נמאסו, that is, "rejected silver." Psalm

106[:24] says, ימסו ארץ הנחמוה, that is, "and they rejected the desirable land." It occurs in the majority of cases that those who are of such a kind are the great, the wealthy, and the famous in this world. Indeed, the Holy Spirit does not regard the external character of the reprobate but the impiety of their hearts and lives. According to this impiety he names them מאסים, whatever else they may be called in this world. Next, it must be noted that he examines it so that we may despise it so much. It is arduous to despise the powerful, the opulent, and the glorious in this world and to consider them as the rejected. One should recognize those who easily are acquainted with the rejected, and those they constantly thrash with their words when they think there is no danger. When it is agreeable for them to enjoy some of their business, they do not flee their fellowship. Indeed, this is not to despise the rejected. It does not say here, "in whose heart," but "in whose eyes" the abominable is despised. It indicates that the pious cannot even see the rejected with patience, still less can they have anything to do with their business. Precaution must be taken here lest we speedily think like the rejected who are guilty in some sins or, thinking that an eagerness for sinning is greater in others than in ourselves, we condemn in the manner of do-gooders and hypocrites. It is fitting that whoever sins with no regard to correcting himself cannot judge that he is not rejected or short of being rejected, for he ignores whether someone is receiving an admonition or not. Whoever can receive an admonition even if he may not immediately obey in all things ought not to be supposed as rejected. The hypocrites among the Jews were condemning sin not in themselves but in others—having eyes for observing the lives of others but being blinder than a mole in regard to their own. Next, it was not fitting that sinners were not concerned about the correction of their own sins, but in that very eagerness—nay more, that opinion—they were thinking that they satisfied true justice if they neither ate nor drank with publicans and sinners. Indeed, they condemned those who were eating and drinking with those sorts of people, just as they also rejected Christ with that same name (Matt. 9[:10–12]). Therefore, let us, as we imitate Christ more than the Pharisees, certainly detest sin and turn away from the rejected. Let us also take care that we simultaneously truly despise the rejected and receive sinners who do not yet despair of Christ. In sum, let us in this way turn away from a partnership with sinners: first, so that we may detest the sin itself; second, so that we may not strengthen in evil those who are sinning; third, so that we may not be infected by the thought of them; and fourth, so that those who are ashamed may be converted.

## Observation

*And who fearing the* L*ORD glorify him.* We observe here that those who are the opposites of the rejected are called those who fear God. We are admonished here that the root of all goodness and righteousness is the fear of God, and, if that is absent, the result is a reprobate and abominable life. He says that whoever fears the Lord will do good things. Next, it must be noted that he calls them fearers of God because they conduct themselves toward their neighbor rightly, blamelessly, and justly. It must be shown that the fear of God is not only in those things that immediately concern God (that is, the first table of the Decalogue) but also in those things that pertain to one's neighbor. A pious person knows not only that this is from God—namely, to dwell before him piously—but also that those things that pertain to one's neighbor should be examined so that we may dwell with our neighbor justly and candidly. Third, it must be noted here what it requires from us, so that we should not only avoid the reprobate, but also that, fearing God, we should honor him. It is easy to avoid a reprobate person, especially if he should offend us by his malice, but to glorify God while fearing him, this does not exist in many, nor is it so easy to do as is thought, especially for a person who may be repenting on account of the indecency of his former way of life, which was up to this point despicable; or for a person who is living under impious magistrates and obnoxious persecutions, as is evident in the case of Jonathan under Saul (1 Sam. 19 and 20), in the case of Obadiah under Ahab (1 Kings 18[:2–16]), or at other times in this world when believers are despised and downcast. Furthermore, during the reigns of Saul, Jeroboam, Ahab, and Manasseh, glorifying God while fearing God was closely connected with peril, and this situation is juxtaposed with those who lived during the reigns of David, Hezekiah, and Josiah. To glorify someone is to consider him precious, to delight in his fellowship, to uphold his reputation, to help meet his needs—all of which can scarcely be done without danger in this world. To honor the dead saints, as seems to be done in the papacy, is both easy and beyond danger. There is nothing they say or do that exasperates the world. Therefore, by honoring the pious, we declare how we love God. We honor not only those who continually lived righteously, but also those who, now first by the correction of their life and then by repentance for their offences, begin to declare that they fear God. The fear of God not only pleases the believer who has continued for a considerable time, but also the new and recent believer. Nothing of all the things we love makes us smile so immediately like seeing those who are just beginning in the fear of God. Next, we honor not only those who fear God who are of renown in the world, but also those held to be obscure and downcast, just as gold, even if it is cast into the mud, is gathered up and considered precious when it is recognized. Third, we glorify not only those pious who bide their time securely and under pious magistrates, but also those who are oppressed under the tyranny of wicked men, and we honor them when they are in danger. Whoever earnestly amasses gold not only gathers what he can obtain without danger, but also what is located in a dangerous place.

## Observation

*He swears to his neighbor and does not change.* First, let us consider that he does not simply say, "he promises to his neighbor and does not change," but rather, "he swears to his neighbor and does not change." Therefore, would a citizen of the kingdom of God be permitted to change without offense to God if he should merely promise something to his neighbor in simple words without an oath? By no means. This is not treated here by the prophet, but he examines the reverence of the divine name that he saw grow flabby and cold in his own time in Israel. Because of this he handed down those predictions to the people, as also below in Psalm 24[:3–6]. He composed psalms of this sort completely for the edification of the church of God and gave predictions to her. He was composing the majority of these for her edification, for the daily admonition of errors, and for inspiring her to a solid eagerness for true piety.

Next, it must be observed that he does not say, "he swears to God and does not change," but rather, "he swears to his neighbor and does not change." This expression has been accommodated to the necessity of the church of those times. The Jews used to assign little value to it if they did not keep what they swore to their neighbor, but they would keep what they vowed to God. Thus, he rightly placed this clause as: "He swears to his neighbor and does not change." He considers only the zeal for the religion of God and his truth so that because of the religion of the name of God and his truth he does not wish to change what he vowed to his neighbor. In our time, we think that if a pious man and citizen of the kingdom of God should keep good faith with his neighbor, whoever he may be, then how much more should he keep good faith with his magistrate, and next, besides that, how much more fully with the Lord God? After the completion of the commentary on the Psalms, we will consider the oath as well as usury in the appendix.

## Explanation

### Verse 5

*Whoever does not give his money at usury, and does not accept a bribe against the innocent. Whoever does these things will not be moved forever* (cf. Ex. 22[:25–27]; Lev. 25[:36–37]; and Deut. 23[:19–20]). It was a provision of the law that no one among the people of God may demand usury from his neighbor. This kind of command protected against the eagerness of avarice and a spirit, favoring a lawyer's, which demands the necessities of one's neighbors without any respect to their benefit. Because they were devoid of faith and the love of God (even in this matter the majority were delinquent just as one may see in Ezekiel 18 and 22 and Nehemiah [5], which is 2 Esdras chapter 5), even David, discerning that this disease of avarice was increasing in intensity in his own time, inserted this little bit in this psalm against usury, admonishing the person who would give his money for usury that it should have no place in the kingdom of God.

*He does not accept a bribe against the innocent.* He mixes together magistrates, judges, advocates, and other similar sorts in this place. The gift of judging is given to mortals by God, and what has been given is so excellent that it should be a help to the innocent and should suppress the ploys of the reprobate. Those things cannot be done if there is either an eagerness to do favors or if greed draws near. For that reason we read in Exodus 23[:8] and Deuteronomy 16[:18–19] that "you shall appoint judges and magistrates in all your city gates that the Lord your God will give to you, throughout each of your tribes, so that they may judge the people with a just judgment and not turn aside toward one party. You shall not consider on the basis of a person or gifts. Because bribes blind the eyes of the wise and alter the words of the just." It does not say, "Perhaps it will not blind the eyes of the wise," but rather he says affirmatively, "Because bribes blind the eyes of the wise and alter the words of the just;" nor does he say, "the eyes of the stupid," but of the wise; nor does he say, "the words of the unjust," but "of the just."

In order to see how corrupt the judgments would have been among the people of Israel, see Psalm 26:10 below, as well as Isaiah 1[:23], Ezekiel 22[:6–12], and Micah 3[:1–3]. It is not against reason that the prophet expels this evil from the citizens of the kingdom of God. He knew that it would prevail excessively among those who were entrusted with the power to judge.

*Whoever does these things will not be moved forever.* This is the conclusion of the psalm in which he promises true felicity to those who do these things, affirming that they would abide in the tabernacle of God and would dwell on his holy mountain. In this way, the psalm begins: "O LORD, who will abide in your tabernacle, who will dwell on your holy mountain?" Therefore, he adds the following: "Whoever walks blamelessly, does righteousness," and so forth. With these things enumerated, as a thorough response he says, "whoever does these things will not be moved forever," on behalf of him that would say, "whoever does these things will abide in my tabernacle and will dwell on my holy mountain." It is understood that the pious will continually remain on the holy mountain of God in such a way that they would never be sent away from it. This is why he says, of course, "he will not be moved forever."

## Observation

### Verse 5

*Whoever does not give his money at usury.* In this place, because the Lord prohibited usury (*usura*) among the people of Israel in his law, two things must be noted. The malice of human nature, by which it occurs that usury has the appearance of a kindness and it is perverted into an inconveniencing and ruining thing. To give money by a loan to a neighbor has the appearance of kindness. If done rightly, it is a kind of true kindness. However, if it should approach usury, then the kindness is perverted into viciousness. For this reason, it is called in the Hebrew נשך, which has the suggestion of being stung. Ultimately, the usury stings, though it seemed to confer a benefit at first. Whoever lends his money to a neighbor certainly does not appear to wish to inflict upon him a financial loss but appears to look out for his financial affairs. When usury is being offered, what at first seemed a work of charity and a help to the necessities of a neighbor, in the end turns by changed sails into avarice and the neighbor's detriment.[6]

The other thing that must be observed concerns the wonderful philanthropy of God by which it is that he cannot bear those practices that obstruct human necessities and undermine an eagerness for kindness among his people. He bountifully lavishes a copious interest (*usura*) on those who tend fields. Meanwhile, he cannot bear the fact that interest (*usura*) is exacted from the one to whom money is given and, in return, charity is wounded. The farmer who commits his seed to the ground for interest (*usura*) does not sin. However, whoever gives his money to his neighbor for interest does sin.

The greedy man says here: "Therefore, I will keep my money for myself, and concerning that point I will not give my neighbor anything, lest I should fall into the sin of usury." I respond: Do not give money to your neighbor that is subject to usury, but rather give according to his interest (*usura*). Give simply without interest, if you wish to flee the force of the sin of usury. Nor should you say, "Who commands that I should give money (which is mine) to others without respect to my advantage?" If you are a Jew, by the authority of the law of God you are compelled to give your money to your destitute brother without usury, concerning which see Deuteronomy 15[:7–11]. Whereas if you are a Christian, you must hear the voice of Christ in Matthew 5[:22]

6. Musculus alludes to the piratical tactic of flying misleading sails to lure and lull a merchant into a false sense of security. When within striking distance, and when the merchant is without chance of escape, the pirate vessel springs its true colors and swoops in on the merchant vessel.

in which he says, "Whoever seeks from you, give to him; and willingly, without you receiving anything in return, do not turn him away." In Luke 6[:30] he says, "Give, hoping for nothing in return from him." Therefore, even if he does not fall into the vice of usury, whoever denies his money to his neighbor still falls into the sin of cruelty, and in the same way is rendered disobedient against God just as if he gave his money for usury.

## Observation

*And he does not accept a bribe against the innocent.* It must be noted here what he does not say, "and he does not accept a bribe from the innocent," but rather, "he does not accept a bribe against the innocent." Whoever are guiltless, relying on the case that they consider good and just, do not think it is necessary for them to influence the judge with bribes in order that he might judge rightly. Besides, whoever offers bribes to a judge beckons him to do this to corrupt that judge and charm him away from the path of righteousness, which does not belong to those who know that justice should stem from themselves. Therefore, he says rightly, "and he does not accept a bribe against the innocent."

Next, it must also be observed that he does not simply say, "and he does not accept a gift," but rather, "and he does not accept a gift against the innocent." In itself it is not evil to accept gifts, just as it is not evil to give gifts. However, to accept gifts in such a way that judgment is perverted against the guiltless is all that is rejected by the Holy Spirit, who requires such integrity in judges that even if they should be given gifts, yet they do not wish to depart the width of a fingernail from that which is fair and just.

Third, it also must be considered that if someone who accepts bribes against the innocent sins, then certainly someone who offers bribes to the judge against the innocent sins no less. Next, if someone sins by leading some private person away by gifts from the path of righteousness to sin, then how much more does someone sin who attempts to corrupt either a public minister of the truth of God or a public minister of justice, for these ministers are a certain common good and, because their integrity is for the benefit of the many, their destruction is such a public perversity. The perversion of judges is an utmost curse. In this place, water is sought and fire is found; justice is sought and both injustice and violence are found; life is sought and death is found; as much audacity as you please to pillage and defraud is furnished to the shameless so that they manage from this cause not only to be slaves to their own avarice and malice, but also this audacity is imparted to patrons, advocates, judges, and to quibbling lawyers. Wherefore it prevails that there are no courts other than corrupt ones. Clearly a lust for bribes is so great a curse if it should occupy the mind of judge that it was not without reason that Jehoshaphat prohibited the judges from it with such great earnestness (2 Chron. 19[:5–7]).

Fourth, neither do I think that policy should be transgressed. If, in secular matters such great integrity is required of judges and magistrates so that they are not allowed to corrupt themselves with bribes against the innocent, what must be said about bishops who through bribes dispense nearly everything in the church, and by receiving bribes sell the flock of the Lord to wolves and to the impious? There are a great number, when the simoniac heresies are condemned, who either by request, by price, or by allegiance dispense sacred orders. I ask you, what place do they have in the kingdom of God?

## Observation

*Whoever does these things will not be moved forever.* It must be observed that he does not say, "whoever knows these things," "whoever reads these things," "whoever sings these things," "whoever preaches these things," but, "whoever does these things." Therefore, not only is an acquaintance with true righteousness required, but also a true and solid observance of it. See Matthew

7[:24], “Whoever hears my words … and does them,” as well as James 1[:22], “You shall be doers of the word, not only hearers.”

Next, consider that he says, “he will not be moved forever.” This place pertains to the perpetuity of that true happiness that exists in the kingdom of God. There are in this life many citizens of the kingdom of God who are not true ones, but painted as such, who will not remain in the kingdom of God but will perish (see my commentary on Psalm 1[:6] above and Psalm 37[:1–2, 9–10, 35–36, 38] below), just as tares do not always remain among the grain, but at harvest time they are cast out (Matt. 13[:24–43]). Moreover, the true citizens will remain in this world even though they may be assailed by many and great temptations (Matt. 7[:25–27]). It does not say, “whoever does these things will not be tempted or assailed,” but, “he will not be moved forever.” In such a way, the truly pious and citizens of the kingdom of God are divinely guarded so that they cannot be subverted and destroyed. They can be slaughtered, but they cannot be moved out of the kingdom of God. Thus, those who boast about their knowledge of the truth and kingdom of God only when some tempest breaks violently on them should not hope for the future, that they should persist immovably. They will not persist unless they strive for justice from their heart and truly reach for the kingdom of God.

# Concerning the Oath*

Here at the end of our commentary on Psalm 15, we are now adding by way of an appendix those things that should have been addressed above, now that, by the grace of the Lord, the whole work has been completed. Why was it not done above? (I do not think that a reason should be given at all, especially when this oversight can be mended easily enough.) In the commentary on Psalm 15, it was neglected by a lack of due consideration (something that lurks in large and prolix works). In the last two verses of Psalm 15, the prophet requires, among other things, this kind of integrity from a citizen of the kingdom of God—namely, that he neither changes what he swore to his neighbor nor gives his money to him for usury. Therefore, it would be worthwhile to annotate something concerning both oath-taking and usury, especially because in our day everything is filled with oaths and because usury has grown to such an enormous extent. I know

* This treatise is the first of two appendices to the commentary on Psalm 15. This translation is based on Wolfgang Musculus, *In Davidis Psalterium sacrosanctum Commentarij: In quibus et reliqua catholicae religionis nostrae Capita passim, non praetermissis orthodoxorum etiam Patrum sententijs, ita tractantur, ut Christianus lector nihil desiderare amplius possit* (Basel: Herwagen, 1573), 1129–37.

full well that those kinds of people who, up to this point, are far away from the integrity of Christian piety such that they are not even possessed by any reverence for the divine name—much less motivated by an internal spirit of charity—do not have ears to hear. Indeed, lest I should abandon the duty of being a faithful admonisher, I will admonish simply and candidly a pious person concerning what he should realize and to what things he should attend.

It is not necessary that I should define what an oath is. It is rather well-known and customary that it requires a declaration. An oath is that in which, with God as a witness by a citation of his name, either we testify about the truth of something, or, because it is imposed, we inviolably promise that we will guard ourselves. We are speaking not about a frivolous matter but about a legitimate oath.

The rationale for an oath is this: It is presumed that there exists in all mortals the belief that there is a divinity to whom (1) all secret things are open; (2) by whom trust as well as truth are most highly esteemed; and, conversely, to whom (3) treachery, fraud, and falsehood are exceedingly displeasing. It is the pursuit of righteousness that punishes perjurers with a deserved vengeance, maintained by the public use, so that we may use the name of this divinity, the God of all, for the purpose of testifying in order to produce belief in those things whose truth we cannot render certain and resolute without some pact. We also appoint God as the avenger if we should either swear something falsely or not render what was promised. Concerning that point, all are convinced that it is not allowed that an abuse of God's name should go unpunished. The duty of this sort of oath-taking existed perpetually from the beginning, especially by our ancestors, not only among the Jews, but also among the heathen nations. By taking an oath, those things that are doubtful and uncertain are confirmed. Also, if something arises that is disputed, it is settled by the intervention of an oath. For this reason, the apostle says in Hebrews 6[:16], "People vow by one greater than they are, and the end of every controversy is at the confirmation of oaths." There is nothing obscure about these things. Therefore, they do not need a broader disclosure, but we must advance to those things about which there is more debate—namely, first, whether or not it is permitted for Christians to take an oath; second, what is an abuse of an oath; and third, concerning the dissolution of oaths.

## Whether the Use of Oaths Is Permitted for Christians

This question would not be necessary if the Anabaptists in our time had not thrown the consciences of many into confusion by that erroneous doctrine by which they strive to destroy absolutely every oath from the public, as if oaths were illicit. Thus, they do this by the pretext of Christ's words in Matthew 5[:33–37] in which he says, "On the contrary you have heard that the ancients had said, 'you will not swear falsely, but you will pay to the Lord what you have vowed.' But I say to you, you shall not swear at all, neither by heaven, because it is the throne of God, nor by earth because it is his footstool ... but your speech will be such that your yes is yes and your no is no. Furthermore, whatever is adjoined beyond these things proceeds from the evil one." From these words they gather that, for a Christian, any kind of oath is entirely forbidden on account of this little universal expression "at all," which they consider a prohibition against anyone swearing in any way. Indeed, how poorly they understand the words of Christ and infer from them this doctrine, I will state later. Moreover, it appears that it should be shown at the present whether an oath made without treachery against the truth and made with the sanction of the divine name is a thing in itself evil and illicit or not. If it is evil in itself, then swearing will by all means also be illicit. If it is not evil, then neither will it be illicit, unless it is rendered evil and illicit by the circumstances of the oath. If anyone should speak evil on account of an oath, then it is evil necessarily because by swearing he sins either against the glory of the name of God or against the love of neighbor. If indeed he does not sin by swearing in either way so that neither the love of God nor the love of neighbor is injured, I do not see how it can be said with some kind of right and firm reason that oath-taking must be evil and illicit.

## Oath-Taking Is Not Against the Glory of God

First, if that rationale should be considered on account of which throughout the whole world and among all nations the employment of oath-taking has prevailed, which is beyond memory, it will be evident (in my opinion) that it does not in any way detract from the glory of God, because the truth is confirmed by the usage of his name and it procures trust. Otherwise, who knows what the truth is, with no other means, either by witnesses or proof, except through the usage of the name of God to produce something trustworthy? As a matter of fact, because God is truth itself, it cannot be the case that he painfully endures this custom because in such testimony the truth of his name is asserted. Such reverence and awe does not cause dishonor to his name since, by being sworn in the case of an obscure and uncertain matter, it is not believed on account of the person swearing but because of the reverence for the divine name used in the oath-taking. That reverence and awe felt first by those swearing and then by those to whom the oath is offered, is that God alone is the knower of secret and hidden things and the hater and avenger of all treachery. No sensible person is so insane as to think that a disgrace has been done to their own name if everywhere it should be demanded as a testimony of the truth and it alone had authority among everyone, so that by the citation of that name even by others it should be considered as a trust without any contradiction from others. How plainly insane would a person be if they should not recognize that any use of the oath, provided that levity and lies are removed, does not subtract anything from the glory of God, but in fact adorns it. Thus, in Jeremiah 4[:2] we read: "And you will swear, as the LORD lives, in truth, in judgment, in righteousness, and those nations will bless and praise him." How do the nations praise the Lord through that which his people swear by his name? They praise him, that is, they render his name glorious, when by swearing they have that trust, and they discern in the one swearing only his reverence and his watchfulness, so that what he swore, he should also render that very thing. Why did not the prophet simply say, "you will swear, as the LORD lives," but rather he added, "in truth, judgment, and righteousness"? Because it is also used both in the binding of oneself to God and it conveys the cause for giving glory to the name of the Lord. You shall be confident not simply, but supremely, that it is good. Good, I say, in itself, if it is rightly used.

## Oath-Taking Is Not Contrary to Love of One's Neighbor

The apostle's passage from Hebrews 6[:16], which we have cited above, declares sufficiently enough that the use of an oath in human affairs frequently suffices, because through its use it imposes an end to controversies. "The oath is the end of every controversy," he says, and tends toward the establishment of truth and peace. As a matter of fact, to the extent that disagreements, quarrels, contentions, brawls, and other such things perturb human affairs, they also destroy the greatest good of peace from a community. Also, whoever is either the author of contentions and disagreements, or, from another direction, the one who offers the kindling to provoke disagreements and also impedes the reconciliation of those who disagree, is considered not without cause a most harmful person and an enemy of human affairs. Therefore, it is essential to determine what is that advantageous and amicable thing in human matters that, by its use, removes disagreements and contentions from the community, confirms the truth, restores peace, and brings back tranquility. When those things are accomplished by the benefit of an oath, which is used piously and reverently in truth and in good faith, who is the sort of person who does not see that the advantage of an oath is so great that it cannot be withdrawn from human affairs without great detriment? Therefore, the necessity of the oath not only proclaims that they are acting exceedingly foolishly (lest what I should say rather sternly be understood insufficiently), but also proclaims how much damage those who labor to subvert absolutely every use of an oath try to foist upon human association. Even if on no account does an oath concern the glory of the name of God, nevertheless to the extent that God loves mankind, their attempt cannot please him in any pact when they strive against it with as much as is in them and try to subvert the tranquility of a public good. Now, the condition of a legitimate oath is such that it is not only beneficial and necessary to human affairs, but also for the singular reason that the glory of the name of God should be adorned among the nations. We irresistibly conclude that its use is not so much evil and illicit as it is proven to be both good and necessary.

## An Oath Is Commanded by God

Although it may not abundantly suffice for a contentious person in adjudicating this question, if one should really inquire, as follows, into the nature and rationale of legitimate oath-taking, then it has been set forward in such a way that (1) not only does it not contain anything evil or illicit, but (2) it also attends to the glory of the name of God, and simultaneously (3) to the most benefit and tranquility in human affairs. Nevertheless, we adduce furthermore that the use of the oath is, in addition to these things, commended in the Holy Scriptures: (1) by what has been handed down by the commandment of God to his people, (2) by the examples of the most pious persons, (3) because it is a certain part of divine worship, and (4) because it has been predicted in the prophets' prophecies concerning the time of the

New Testament that the nations converted to the faith would swear in the name of God. That the commandment to take an oath is from God, see Exodus 22[:7–8, 10–11] where we read: "If anyone should entrust money or equipment into the care of his friend and the money or equipment are carried away by a thief from the recipient, if the thief is found, he will repay double. If the thief escapes unnoticed, the master of the house will come near to the gods"—that is, the magistrates and judges—"and he will swear that he did not stretch out his hand into his neighbor's things, to perpetrate a fraud." "Likewise, if anyone should entrust any ass, bull, or mule into his neighbor's care, and it should die or be debilitated, or be taken by enemies, and no one saw it, then he must take an oath in public that he did not extend his hand to his neighbor's thing. The master of the mule will accept the oath and will not compel his neighbor to pay him back." Therefore, the use of oath-taking has been commended not only in such a way by its quality, but also by the commandment of God, so that it is a fanatical person who wishes to remove it as if he is destroying a reprehensible thing from the community and wishes to cut off things that calm human affairs.

## The Oath Is Commended by the Examples of the Most Pious Fathers

Abraham, who is not only the father of many nations, but also the father of believers in Christ, blamelessly used an oath, as is evident from Genesis 21[:22–24] where we read thus: "At the same time, Abimelech and Phicol, the leader of his army, said to Abraham, 'God is with you in everything that you do. Therefore, swear by God that you will not harm me, my posterity, and my descendants, but equally the mercy which I have done for you, you will do for me, and the lands in which you have dwelt as a foreigner.' And Abraham said, 'I will swear.'" And a little while after that: "Therefore, that place was called Beersheba, because there both of them swore and entered into a covenant of an oath before the well" [Gen. 21:31]. In a similar way, in Genesis 26[:31] we read about Isaac, who also by furnishing an oath entered into a covenant with Abimelech. Thus also Jacob swore to his own father-in-law (Gen. 31[:44]). David, a man following after God's heart, entered a covenant with Jonathan by the interposition of an oath (1 Sam. 20[:17]) and afterward (1 Sam. 24[:21–22]) he also swore to Saul. These examples of such eminent men adequately overcome the Anabaptists. An oath has nothing in itself, if it is rightly used, that displeases God, and it is suitable to a pious man who is beloved of God. Therefore, it is entirely inevitable that the Anabaptists, those defamers of a holy oath—nay, even more, those who have been deluded in such a way that they do not see that they condemn the things with which the elect, gathered from every compass point,[1] are at ease, whose piety and faith is set forth in the Scriptures for us to imitate—are the most separated from these things.

## The Oath Is a Certain Part of Divine Worship

If for a brief moment those things that we have said up to this point concerning an oath are reflected upon—namely, that it pertains to the glory of God and the advantage of our neighbor, it has been commanded by God for his people, and was in use by the holy fathers—let us proceed now to greater things. Therefore, in addition, oath-taking also has this encomium in the Scriptures because it pertains to the worship of God. In Deuteronomy 6[:13] we read: "You will fear the Lord your God, you will serve him alone, and by his name you will swear." In Deuteronomy 10[:20] we read similarly: "You will fear the Lord your God, and you will serve him, you will cling to him, and you will swear in his name." In these two places, not only is oath-taking commanded by God by the encouragement to offer it in the name of God,

1. *cum quibus electi ab Oriente, Occidente, Meridie, ac Septentrione congregati*: lit. "with which the elect, gathered from the East, West, South, and North, ..."

but it is also conjoined to the fear of God, to clinging to him, and to the worship of God because those things are consistent with the nature of oath-taking. From which cause we are readily admonished that oath-taking through the offered usucaption[2] of God's name is of the spirit of fearing and worshipping God, and is inseparable from clinging to him. Moreover, what sane person does not understand that in this way fear, service, and clinging to him pertains to the worship of God, so that every observance and obligation of God, which is, as it were, the root of all of these that can be required for the sincere worship of God, is principally situated in these things? At this point, that also pertains to what is said in Isaiah 19[:18–19], when the prophet wishes to predict that Egypt in part would be led to the knowledge and worship of the true and only God, and that it would happen that five cities in Egypt would swear by the Lord of hosts, and would raise in the middle of Egypt an altar to the Lord, and a monument to the Lord close to its boundaries, which is a sign and testimony to the Lord of hosts in the land of Egypt. Here we also see that the prophet conjoins an oath made under the name of the true God to the worship of God. Moreover, he was persuaded that the worship of God is the obligatory part of oath-taking, by which means those swearing were holding their hands on the altars of their gods, to whom also is covenanted what we read in Exodus 23[:13]: "All the things which I have said to you, keep, and you will not swear by the name of foreign gods, nor will it be heard from your mouth." And Joshua 23:[7–8]: "So that, after you will have entered into the nations, which will be among you, you will not swear in the name of their gods, serve them, or adore them, but rather, you will cling to the LORD your God. Therefore that person who has done these things has turned back from the true

2. Usucaption is the legal concept of acquiring possession through long, undisturbed use. For a standard definition as utilized in the Christian era of the Roman Empire and up to Musculus' time, see *Corpus Iuris Civilis, Institutiones* II.6.

God to swear by those who are not gods." We plainly read what is also said in Jeremiah 5[:7] by God: "Your sons have abandoned me, swearing to those who are not gods." Indeed, what is more useful than the prophetic testimonies? Did not a plain proof of this matter become clear in the case that, when the cult of the dead saints grew up, the people simultaneously began to invoke the saints and conjoin their names to the name of God in the form of an oath?

## An Oath Offered in the Faith of God, in Truth, and in Judgment Is a Certain Mark of the New Testament

So that some contentious person might not resist and say, "those things which have been said up to this point had their place in the Old Testament, but to be sure, however, it is not the case in the New Testament," therefore, it is necessary that those things which were previously mentioned about oath-taking should be proven from the New Testament Scriptures. By such subterfuge, the Anabaptists also try to escape so that they may not be compelled to raise their hands in defeat.[3] Come, let us see by what testimonies their opinion can be overcome and that the use of oath-taking, offered under the name of the one and only true God especially pertain to New Testament times. Moreover, it is my opinion that you will not poison any sincere Christian by going to those things that are foretold in the prophetic predictions concerning the kingdom of Christ as they extend without any contradiction to the New Testament and are most becomingly used by believers in Christ. Therefore, let us hear the prophetic predictions concerning this case. We read in Isaiah 45[:21–23] that God says as follows: "There is not a just and saving God besides me. Turn to me and you, O ends of all the earth, will be

3. *ne manus victi dare cogantur*: lit. "lest they should be compelled to give the hand of the defeated." The imagery is similar to that of a wrestling match where the defeated opponent taps out.

saved because I am God, and there is no other. By myself I have sworn, a word of righteousness will proceed from my mouth, and it will not be turned back because every knee will bow, and every tongue will swear." This prediction relates to the times of the New Testament and to the kingdom of Christ the Savior. First, those words sufficiently declare that not only are the Israelites called to the knowledge and worship of God, but also all the ends of the earth as well. The future is also predicted—namely, that the word progresses from the mouth of God and does not return void, but at every point prospers, in order that every knee will bend to God and every tongue will swear to him—that is, when all nations would recognize, worship, adore, and, after they have left behind their false gods, would swear by his name, and in that way would declare that they had converted to him. This text does not harmonize with anything except the kingdom of Christ and the New Testament, under which, through the preaching of the gospel all the nations of the earth, who existed in the Old Testament time as aliens to the true God, are converted to the true God (Eph. 2[:11–21]). Next, the apostolic writings attest this itself (Rom. 14[:17–19]; Phil. 2[:10–11]) where the prediction under consideration is adapted to the kingdom of Christ. A similar passage is considered in Isaiah 65[:16] where we read as follows: "He who will bless you in the land, he will bless you in the true God, and he who will swear, he will swear by the true God." Moreover, that whole chapter pertains to the calling of the Gentiles and the rejection of the Jews. Therefore, the apostle also employed the testimony of that fact. So, in those prophetic and apostolic testimonies (so beautifully harmonious among themselves), their contentious argument is answered with sufficient clarity. It is also undeniably proven that their trifling results in a fleeing retreat for the Anabaptists, who dispute the use of a legitimate oath in the Old Testament in such a way that in the New Testament an oath must be considered illicit, when, as it were, an oath is a mark of the true knowledge of God and a testimony of the divine worship, eminently pertaining to the New Testament.

## God, Christ His Son, and the Apostles Used an Oath

Because the obdurate Anabaptists with great impudence do not yield to the examples of the fathers—of Abraham, Isaac, Jacob, and David, which we adduced above—but attribute those things to the Old Testament, and annul the imitation of them in the time of the New Testament, let us introduce the examples of those whom, without manifest impiety, they could neither include in the Old Testament times nor exclude from the New Testament times. They have confessed that it is unavoidable that the Lord is not only the Lord of the Jews but also of the Gentiles. God is not only the Lord and author of the Old Testament but also of the New Testament. Next, Christ his Son—although, as Paul says, Christ would come as a minister of circumcision [Rom. 15:8]—yet he is the mediator and chief person (*princeps*) of the New Testament, and so also Paul was not a minister of the circumcision and of the Old Testament, but an incomparable minister to the Gentiles of the New Testament and of the gospel of Christ. Thus, we will consider the examples of God, Christ, and Paul (if any kind of mortal is appropriate for Christians when the first two are sufficient). Therefore, let us see whether or not the use of an oath is appropriate for God, his Son Christ, or any apostle as their minister.

First, many passages in Scripture witness to the fact that God has sworn. In Genesis 22[:16–18]: "'By myself I swear,' says the Lord, 'because you have done this thing, and you have not spared your only-begotten son, I will bless you.'" In Psalm 89[:3, 35]: "I have sworn to David my servant," and, "Once I have sworn in my holiness." In Psalm 95[:11]: "to whom I swore in my wrath." In Psalm 110[:4]: "The Lord swore and he will not repent." In Psalm 132[:11]: "The Lord swore to David the truth." Many such testimonies are read in the writings of the prophets. Moreover because God swears by himself, hence it occurs that the apostle declares in Hebrews 6[:13–16]: "Since he does not have anyone greater by whom he may swear, he swears by himself. Indeed, people swear by him who is greater than themselves." In that passage, it is sufficiently declared that the only distinction placed between people and God is in the cause and use of the oath. It is lawful for both to use an oath, yet people do not swear by themselves but by him who is greater than themselves, that is, by God. God, indeed, does not swear by anyone greater, but rather swears by himself—not because it is illicit in itself to swear by the greater person if there could be one greater than him (but there cannot be), but because he does not have anyone greater than himself by whom he could swear. Therefore, for this reason they should not turn their backs on the challenge and say, "the apostle speaks concerning people, that is the sons of this age, not concerning Christians and the elect when he says, 'People, indeed, swear by one greater.'" For the apostle does not compare people among themselves—the elect with the sons of this age—but rather, he compares people with God, and he distinguishes between those two in this one thing only, that the former swear by one greater than themselves whereas, indeed, God swears by no one greater but by himself.

Next, if that is not even enough for contentious persons, let us examine the example of the apostle Paul. The apostle writes in 2 Corinthians 1[:23] as follows: "Moreover I call upon God as a witness against my soul that sparing you I would not, in addition, come again to Corinth." These words clearly contain an oath, for he cites God as a witness against his own soul if he is lying, so that he may convince the Corinthians of the truth of those things that he says—of course, for this reason he would not come to Corinth, in addition, so that he might spare them. Here is a most prominent use of an oath, and no sensible person is so dense that he does not see that here Paul has manifestly and expressly used an oath. Nor does Paul fear even to summon God as a witness in other passages, and by the use of God's name, he creates trust in his words, just as it appears in Romans 1[:9], Galatians 1[:8–9], Philippians 1[:8], and 1 Thessalonians 2[:10]. Moreover, he adjures his own Timothy with the gravest supplication, saying, "I implore you before God and Christ Jesus, who shall judge the living and the dead, and by his coming and his kingdom, preach the word!" (2 Tim. 4[:1–3]). Whoever would adjure another person—and that a brother and fellow-minister[4]—to such a degree with an awe-inspiring entreaty, by what reason in a similar instance would he have recoiled from offering an oath? Therefore, if you should note the example of the apostle to that degree (and he is a strong example of a minister of the New Testament), it is evident that the Anabaptists are exceedingly impudent when they contend that the use of an oath is not lawful for Christians.

Third, let us proceed to Christ himself, and let us see whether or not he uses an oath. As often as he said, "Amen, amen, I say to you," then just as often he swore by himself, even if he did not expressly summon the name of God. In fact, the force of the oath is not only in some expression in the name of God, but also in those things that concern the glory of God, just as the truth properly relates to God, and concerns his glory. Moreover, that expression "Amen, amen I say to you," is nothing other than, "Truly, truly I say to you, by the truth I affirm to you." For instance, the expression *Amen* is supposed for the truth, just as it is familiar to whoever knows Hebrew. Paul also used that expression in 2 Corinthians 1[:20] when he said the promises of God are in Christ "yes" (ναὶ) and "amen." Therefore, to all the pious, it is taboo to use this lightly because they realize that it has the force of an oath. If they rashly use this little expression, "truly," it is just as if they should summon God himself as a witness. Thus, Paul in Hebrews 6[:14] introduces God as swearing by himself, saying: "ἦμην εὐλογῶν εὐλογήσω σε," that is, "truly

4. *symmista* (Gk. συμμύστης), from the classical Latin of *symmysta*: a fellow colleague in the priesthood, a fellow priest.

and by no means uncertainly, blessing I shall bless you." The little expression ἦμην expresses the same thing in Greek as τὸ ὄυτως, that is, "actually." So, for this formula of swearing, the Son of God the Father, who is equal in all things and also has none greater by whom he might swear, skillfully constructed his own oaths. Christ, who is the most suitable of all persons, even frequently swears by himself and says, "truly, truly I say to you," from which it is evident without any contradiction not only that God the Father swore, but also Christ the Son swore time after time.

Consequently, it cannot be denied that an oath is not unlawful (because it is not evil, on the contrary it is good). An oath works for the glory of the name of God and the advantage of our neighbors. It has been commanded by God and has been employed by the most pious fathers. Next, it is part of the worship of God and a mark of the New Testament foretold by the predictions of the prophets. Finally, God swore, the apostle Paul swore, and Christ himself swore. On account of all of this, who does not see that what the same Christ says in Matthew 5[:34]—"Moreover, I say to you, you shall not swear at all"—must not be understood to contradict all those irresistible testimonies of the clear truth, or to oppose not only God the Father, but also Christ himself? On the contrary, it is necessary that we seek the sense that contains no contradiction, and at the same time is consistent with the purpose of the case, which is the course of action supported therein. If the Anabaptists would have used caution and careful consideration here, they would have in no way provoked this question in the church of Christ to throw the consciences of believers into confusion.

## Concerning the Sense of the Words of Christ, "Moreover, I Say to You, You Shall Not Swear at All" (Matt 5[:34])

It is considered by common sense in expounding the Scriptures to be an exceedingly necessary rule that the words are not so much attended to as the intention and way of thinking of the one speaking. Otherwise, if the words are pushed without consideration of the sense in which they are said, it cannot happen but that the interpreter is violently mistaken. For example, in this same chapter, Christ says, "Moreover, I say to you, 'Do not resist an evil person'" [Matt. 5:39]. If you push the words then it will be unlawful to resist evil people in any way. In this way, magistrates, ministers of the word, and the authority of parents toward children are utterly removed from the community, and a most unimpeded course is permitted to evil persons of whatever sorts. In another example, Luke 14[:26] says, "If anyone comes to me and does not hate his father and mother, his brothers and sisters, his wife and children, he cannot be my disciple." If it is contended that the words are clear and evident, what other thing follows than that the commandments about honoring one's parents and about loving one's wife have been abrogated for Christians? Therefore, as they examine it, while they love their enemies, they are also established as haters of parents, brothers, sisters, wives, and children, unless of course they do not wish to be Christians. Matthew 23[:2] says concerning the scribes and Pharisees, "Whatever they should say to you, do it." Therefore, it is concluded that the doctrine of the scribes and Pharisees in all things without distinction should be embraced, so that in vain Matthew 16[:6] says, "Beware of the leaven of the Pharisees," or in John 10[:8] he says, "Whoever came before me were thieves and robbers." Therefore, the prophets and John were thieves and robbers, for they came before Christ! In 1 Corinthians 9[:22], Paul says, "I have become all things to all persons." Therefore, if you push the expression generally, he has become an idolater to idolaters, and in 1 Corinthians 10[:23], "All things are lawful for me." Therefore, it was lawful for him to frequent prostitutes and to commit adultery! See how inappropriate and absurd things can be inferred from the words of Christ and the apostles if they are simply pushed without comprehension of the sense that is intended. This plainly occurs in a very similar way in that place when, in the words of Christ—"Moreover, I say to you, you shall not swear at all"—the expression "at all" is seized without a circumspect manner and their interpretation is deduced from that sense that the rest of the Scriptures taken as a whole resist, and their interpretation opposes not only the deeds of the fathers, but also those of Christ himself and of Paul.

Therefore, just as I have also spoken in regards to Matthew 5[:33–37], where those things are considered, it entirely follows that Christ is not speaking about legitimate oath-taking, but about day-to-day swearing in a habitual and shallow manner, by which expressions we affirm almost everything we say by swearing. That custom also had prevailed among the Jews. They used to swear rashly by heaven, by earth, by the city of Jerusalem, and each person by his own head, and because oaths of this sort were not done by some pronouncement of the name of God, they were persuaded that no one had been obligated by those things to keep what he had sworn or that no one committed an offense if he should have sworn with a spurious pact. This was strengthening that persuasion in the minds of the common people, and secondarily in the minds of the Pharisees and scribes, concerning the commandment of God regarding not swearing, and that verse in Exodus 20[:7]: "You shall not use the name of the LORD your God in vain." They were expounding it in such a way by teaching that if anyone should swear falsely, he is not sinning against the name of God unless he swears by some name of God that is peculiar and proper to him. In such a way, Rabbi Shlomo wrote on this passage in Exodus.[5] The words of Christ

5. Rabbi Shlomo Yitzhaki (1040–1105), also known as Rashi or רש״י, was born in Troyes, France, and was a commentator upon the Babylonian Talmud and the biblical text (or Tanakh). His commentary was included

in Matthew 23[:16–22] sufficiently declare the error of the Jews. For he says as follows:

> Woe to you, you blind leaders, who say, "Whoever should swear by the temple, it is nothing. On the other hand, whoever swears on the gold of the temple, he is obligated." O stupid and blind people! What is greater, the gold or the temple which sanctifies the gold? And, "whoever swears on the altar, it is nothing, but whoever swears on the gift which is on the altar, he is indebted." O you blind people! What is greater, the gift or the altar which sanctifies the gift? Therefore, whoever swears on the altar swears on it and by all things which are upon it. And whoever should swear on the temple swears on that and on him who dwells in the temple. And whoever swears by heaven, swears on the throne of God, and by him who sits upon it.

From these words, it is plainly evident how erroneous was the teaching concerning the oath that the scribes and Pharisees had brought in, which encouraged a false persuasion of the common people. The Lord contradicts this teaching in another place (Matt. 5[:33–37]; 23[:16–22]). He does not destroy the authority of the law, which instructed the legitimate making of an oath, nor does he condemn the examples of the most holy men who had used the oath well, because he is not speaking about the legitimate oath but about the reckless and daily type that was made rashly in daily speech, thoughtlessly by an evil custom of swearing, and with a deceptive persuasion because they were not being held to keep it. They had also not sworn by the name of God, the

in the second edition of the printers David Bomberg and Israel Cornelius Adelkind's *Biblia Rabbinica* (Venice: Bomberg, 1525). For a translation of Rashi's commentary on Psalm 15, see *Rashi's Commentary on Psalms 1-89 (Books I–III)*, trans. Mayer I. Gruber (Atlanta: Scholar's Press, 1998), 97–98; for the Hebrew text, see the Hebrew section of the same, 26–27. See also a complete edition of the entire commentary by M. I. Gruber, *Rashi's Commentary on the Psalms*, Brill Reference Library of Judaism, vol. 18 (Philadelphia: Jewish Publication Society, 2007), 225.

gold of the temple, or the gift on the altar, and so in this sense Christ's words are clear. "The saying is from of old," that is, he is saying, "Thus, it has been handed down from your ancestors by the scribes and Pharisees, 'You shall not swear falsely.'" This law was taught, for Leviticus 19[:12] reads: "You shall not swear falsely in my name; you shall not defile the name of the LORD your God." The scribes had exposited it as follows: "If you should swear falsely by the name of the LORD God, you will be guilty, and you have defiled the name of God. If indeed you should swear falsely, but not by the name of God, then you will not be guilty. For neither have you defiled the name of God." They had added to this law that, "Moreover, you shall pay your vow to the LORD," that is, "If you vowed something by swearing to the LORD God and employed his name, you are obligated to pay it. But less than that, you are not obligated because you swore neither to the LORD nor by his name. Just as if someone is not obligated who swore, not to God, but to his neighbor; he swore not by the name of God, but by some creature."

Therefore, Christ makes it a topic so that he may admonish this pharisaical teaching as below standard: "Moreover, I say to you, you shall not swear at all." In what way? Can it be that you shall not swear even to God? Can it be that you shall not swear even in a trial, in righteousness by the name of God, and in the legitimate form of an oath? Listen, he does not say, "You shall not swear either to God, nor by the name of God, nor in a trial." Why? Because the Jews themselves evidently used to know that a person is not guiltless who might have sworn falsely to God during a trial, who swore falsely under the name of God, and who also swore falsely to his neighbors. It was not necessary to remind them of those things, for he was not speaking about legitimate oaths but about their daily ones, by which (short of using the name of God), they were swearing falsely, with impunity, and without remorse for their sin. Therefore, he says in this way: "Moreover, I say to you, whatever your scribes will have handed down, lest you should swear at all, you will not swear by heaven (because it is God's throne), or by earth (because it is his footstool), or by Jerusalem (because it is the great city of the king), or by your own head (because you cannot even make one hair of your head white or black)." See which formulas of oath-taking he strips away. He says, "Neither by heaven, nor by earth, nor by Jerusalem, nor by your own head." Notwithstanding, no one was using these particular formulas of oath-taking in a trial, no one was using them in covenants, no one was using them in legitimate contracts, no one was using them in the vows that they made to God. In such matters just mentioned, it was vowed by the use of the name of God so that what is actually evident from this is that no one was judged to be held and bound by these oaths that Christ enumerates here. Therefore, they were not legitimate, but the usual ones used in conversation. Next, observe also the reasons that he adds: "You shall not swear," he says, "by heaven." Why? "Because it is the throne of God." "Nor by earth." Why? "Because it is God's footstool." "Nor by Jerusalem." Why? "Because it is the city of the great king." "Nor by your head." Why? "Because you cannot make one hair either black or white." That is, because it is not yours but a work of divine power.

If those oaths contained something of trust, truth, and reverence, by which the name of God might be glorified—just as we have shown above concerning legitimate oath-taking—those reasons might be completely unsuitable. On account of that, swearing would be by heaven, which is God's throne, where the glory of God is illustrated. Also, the rest would relate in such a way, on some account, to the glory of God. Yet if this were the case he would have said, "Swear by heaven, which is God's throne," rather than, "You shall not swear by heaven." Therefore by this consideration it is also sufficiently evident that Christ is not speaking concerning legitimate oaths but about trifling, rash, and day-to-day oaths, which have been employed without trust, reverence, and truth, and, to a greater extent, with contempt for God's throne, God's footstool, and the city of God, as well as the other works of God that were made for his honor. Here and there he does this insofar as he says, "Let your speech be such that your yes is yes and your no is no." This indicates that he is correcting their bad habit in their conversation, in which either in affirming or denying something, they were swearing rashly. He does not say, "Let your vows, let your promises, let your judicial testimonies, and your bail-bonding, and such other things," but rather, "Let your speech be such that your yes is yes and your no is no." It is also in a similar way that he adds, "whatever is beyond these is from the evil one." This is as if to say: "It is because you are not content with these words—yes is yes and no is no—but rather you attach oaths—by heaven, by the earth, by Jerusalem. This occurs because your heart is vain, not furnished with any reverence and respect for God's throne, God's footstool, and the city of God, and because you do not believe anyone unless they swear, because your speech is full of lies and falsities." If we do not understand the words of Christ in this way, how will we respond to Porphyry and Julian if they might construct this calumny against Christ—namely, that it was not the case that in his speech his yes was yes and his no was no, because he so often he would redouble his Amen? For this reason, was that redoubling of it evil? Likewise, in what way will we view the apostle lest he should have written from an evil motive every time he said, "God is my witness," or, "I invoke God as a witness against my soul"? May God forbid that either Christ or his apostle could be charged with such shallowness! Therefore, that error of the Anabaptists is exceedingly dense and senseless, by which coarse and ignorant persons are seduced by deceitful people, and those entering into their midst are not brethren but impostors and scoundrels who do not serve Christ but their own passions. So that I might uncover the wickedness of these people and might run to the aid of those seduced, I have written concerning this very cause in the Germanic dialect, which was printed at Augsburg, a dignified city with many titled persons, in the year 1533.[6] Indeed, since that little book perhaps only fell into the hands of a few, and it could not be understood by those who do not know German, it appears again in this place to serve the public utility, and to address an error not yet extinguished in the church of Christ, either to suppress it according to my moderateness or at least to render it suspect. To the extent of this question, whether the use of oath-taking is lawful for Christians, I have spoken.

## Concerning the Abuse of an Oath

Above all, these two things are necessarily required in asserting the case of the truth at any time. The first thing is that whatever is true in some matter should be declared and asserted. Second, if any abuse should arise, it should be rejected and destroyed. That is to say, it is the lot of truth in this world that either it will be condemned while being unknown by the ignorant, or it will be hijacked by the learned into an abuse. Both have happened in this case regarding oaths. The Anabaptists, because they neither know nor endeavor to learn, obstinately condemn oaths. Carnal persons, destitute of both faith and the religion of God, perversely usurp what they do not condemn. Therefore, in the right order, the truth of legitimate oath-taking was first asserted, next also the abuse of it must be rebuked. After the error of the Anabaptists has been reprehended, we turn to strip away the abuse of the oath. Moreover that abuse is so prolific that I think it is impossible to survey and to shake out all the species of it. Nearly all the things that are done in human life swarm with oaths so that it is necessary on account of the multitude of oaths to land in this case upon those that occur in loquaciousness—those in which sin cannot be avoided. On account of them that are led by reverence for the divine name, I will continuously touch upon

6. *Ain frydsams unnd Christlichs Gesprech ains Evangelischen auff ainer und ains Widerteüffers auff der andern seyten so sy des Aydschwürs halben mitainander thünd* (Augsburg: Philip Ulhardt, 1533).

this part, by which admonitions they can keep their consciences intact, safe from defiling the name of God. For the sake of these things, we will consider how both someone demanding an oath and someone offering an oath abuse the obligation of an oath.

## How They Sin Who Demand an Oath

Those who demand oaths sin in a threefold[7] manner. First, when they set forth an oath for things trivial and of no account, or even from certain persons of doubtful credibility, concerning whom it cannot be believed that they are held by a particular eagerness for the truth and reverence for the divine name. Although no one knows what is in a person except the spirit of the person that is in the person—and the heart of a person is, by itself, inscrutable—yet it cannot be excused when oaths are imposed upon such persons, who by evident proofs show themselves to be light-minded and vain without any faith and fear of God, and altogether the sort from whom no judge (if he concerns himself with the case of offering an oath) summons even the least bit of faith, even if they swear a hundred times as requested. Whoever imposes the guarantee of making an oath upon such persons knowingly offers them an occasion to perjure themselves.[8] Therefore, that levity and indifference (ἀδιαφορία) of whoever rashly imposes the oaths also proves the levity of the judges and magistrates.

Next, it is sin when in a rather vain and insignificant matter without any importance a judge, either for his own sake or incited by a plaintiff, imposes a guarantee of making an oath—namely, by using the name of God. This occurs here and there because

7. Musculus writes "threefold" (*tripliciter*) but actually goes on to describe four ways.

8. This sentence, as well as the marginal reference in the original, refer to Gratian's *Decretum*; see *Corpus Iuris Canonici*, ed. Aemilius Ludouici Richteri (Leipzig: Bernhardi Tauchnitz, 1889), Decreti Pars Secunda, Causa XX, Quaestio V, caput v.

it happens in the majority of the cases when either the truth is investigated and known by other means, or the case of controversy may be settled only to a greater extent by an abridgment than would be desired by a just and full inquiry.

Third, it is wrong when an oath is imposed in an extraordinary or impossible matter, or the kind that a judge knows cannot be offered. For this reason he does not demand an oath so that it might be kept, but so that it might be kept as a convention, or the reason is held as a personal interest. Thus, they err at the present time, whoever demand, as they say, under an oath from priests and monks who have not been castrated, a vow of celibacy and chastity, when by the universal corruption of so many years—indeed of the ages—it clearly has happened that the institution of this sort is kindling for every sort of wantonness and impurity. It is also the sort of oath-taking that is required from the suffragan bishops, so that they must convert those churches, under whose titles they are ordered, to faith in Christ by the preaching of the gospel. That case is not of such a kind that what they swear is even possibly believed, nor is this requested in earnest, but, on the contrary, a vain and frivolous oath is knowingly and skillfully imposed from which at last the wretches are absolved in appearance so that they may continue rather carefree in their sin. How much better, I ask, concerning this matter is that elector of Mainz, who falsely calls himself the Bishop of Sidon, should he have written about the imaginary sacrifice of the papist Mass, if he should decide to conduct himself as a good man and devoted to the truth?[9]

Fourth, they sin in the form of the oath, who conjoin the names of the saints to the name of God, for they give a reason

9. Michael Helding was the titular Bishop of Sidon from 1538 to 1550. Helding, together with Julius von Pflug, bishop of Naumburg-Zeitz, and Johann Agricola, authored the Augsburg Interim in 1548. Helding also published a series of sermons on the Mass, *Von der hailigsten Messe* (Ingolstadt: Alexander Weissenhorn, 1548).

for that sin, which Jeremiah 5[:7] blames on the sons of Israel. "Your sons," he says, "abandon me and they swear by those who are not gods." No sensible person among the papists would say that the saints are gods. Therefore, although they may swear by the saints, at any rate they swear by those who are not gods as if they were a witness conscientious of them, which is a sin that is a kind of deficiency. Chrysostom says in his second homily on Matthew, chapter 5 that whoever swears by something that is not God commits idolatry because he deifies that by which he swears.[10] What is it to deify someone with an oath than to attribute to him familiarity with the secrets of the heart—knowing whether something in the promises, assertions, testimonies, and vows of everyone may be true or false—and to say that his is the sort of righteousness and power that exacts punishments suitable to perjured things? If the saints can be responsible for those things, then they can be deservedly deified by the reverence of an oath. If indeed knowledge, justice, and power of all those sorts of things belong to God only, what reasonable person does not see how an oath ought not to be taken in a trial and with justice, except in the name of God only, the knower of all secrets and the avenger of every fraud and treachery? As far as this matter is concerned, this is how they repeatedly sin who impose oaths on others.

## How People Sin by Taking Oaths

The sins of those who swear ought to be considered twofold. First is how they sin in daily conversation by swearing without being urged to affirm something with an oath, but by doing so voluntarily for their own sake. Next is how those who have been

10. This is actually Chrysostom's third homily on Matthew 5 (Homily XVII, sec. 5). See Philip Schaff, ed., *Nicene and Post-Nicene Fathers*, 1st series (Reprint, Peabody: Hendrickson, 2004), 10:120. Musculus edited and translated various editions of Chrysostom's works, including *Opera D. Ioannis Chrysostomi* (Basel: Froben and Episcopius, 1548).

urged to swear something with an oath may sin in a trial. In their daily speech one sins by swearing, first, when something is sworn rashly and without cause, even if it is not sworn falsely. For the name of God is used in vain contrary to the third commandment of the Decalogue and against Christ's admonition where he says, "Moreover, I say to you, you shall not swear at all, but let your speech be such that your yes is yes and your no is no" [Matt. 5:37]. The sexual union of a man and woman is good as it has been instituted by God. Certainly, if it occurs in a legitimate marriage, but it is not so if it occurs outside of marriage. It is good to sing psalms, especially if they are sung to the Lord and with reverence, but it is not good if the psalms are used without any reverence either at dinner parties with drinking or in the churches for profit. Likewise, an oath made under the name of God is good if it is done in a trial and reverently with the fear of the Lord. It is not good if it is done rashly and lightly.

Second, the sin is augmented when something is sworn not only lightly, rashly, and without cause, but also falsely and mendaciously. To lie by itself is evil. The evil is doubled with the accessory of an oath. It was a capital offense among the Egyptians if someone should perjure themselves "by the salvation of Pharaoh." Whoever perjures by the name of God—how could that person be considered guiltless?

Third, a great increase is added to this sin when a neighbor is injured by the perjury. Here are the degrees: the first degree is if a neighbor is injured in his goods, the second is if he is injured in his reputation and in the public esteem, the third is if he is wounded in his body or life, the highest degree is if he is wounded in his soul and in his very salvation.

Thus, those swearing are accustomed to excuse what they do when they are caught. (1) Some say, "I do not swear out of an eagerness for evil but out of habit." This does more to accuse than to excuse them! A habit of this sort is caused not by swearing every now and then, but by the most frequent sort of oath-taking, and it is the argument of a soul destitute of the fear of God. (2) Others in a very similar manner cloak themselves with a multitude of oaths. In a multitude of sins, one magnifies a sin, one does not diminish it. Finally, it provokes the wrath of God because the sin strengthens and ripens. (3) There are those who may say, "No one is inconvenienced by my habit of oath-taking." Reflect on this: you will inconvenience no one if you deny God and serve Satan. Meanwhile, you will destroy yourself. Whoever destroys his own salvation, how could he be held guiltless? Likewise, how does he injure no one if he injures God? Moreover, someone injures God gravely by rashly taking an oath and profaning his name. (4) To the contrary, it is pretended by some that they do not swear by the name of God. Those sorts do not observe the admonition of Christ in Matthew 5[:33–37] in which it is declared that the glory of God is profaned when something is sworn rashly by his creatures. (5) Others say that they do not lie by taking an oath. As if it is enough to excuse their sin if they should not lie but sin by habitual and trivial oath-taking. Therefore, a God-fearing man will most studiously take precautions so that he does not profane the name of God by swearing rashly, because if he should lose control of himself and swear, this does not excuse him but, rather, accuses him, and he should ask that his sin be forgiven by the Lord. I know that certain republics, a little before these years of tribulation and trial, were set up in such a way that if one of their citizens should have sinned by taking an oath with levity, he would have been lawfully punished. Now, indeed, because laws of such holy discipline are broken, just as the former impunity has been restored for whoring, adulteries, drunkenness, usury, and thus also for rash oaths, it is therefore inevitable that soon the implacable wrath of God will flare up against our Germany. God's wrath continuously increases in such a way that the nobles of the peoples will be among the first to be given their just penalties by the Lord God. Nobles, now thinking that they have pursued the tranquility of affairs—I do not know how—because they have thrown off the yoke of the Lord, and being guilty for not enduring any further dangers on account of the gospel of the kingdom of God, prefer not to endure the wrath and indignation of men, whose breath (*flatus*) is in their nostrils, and thus fall into the wrath and indignation of God, whose breath (*spiritus*) shakes the entire globe.

In the second place, it must be considered how they sin who swear in trials. First they sin who swear for the sake of a little money. They ought to quickly bear their destruction who invoke the sacred name of God for the sake of such a vain cost. Next, they sin who consciously and knowingly swear falsely. This is done in two ways: (1) when they assert that something is true that they know is false or when they affirm that something is false that they are well aware is true; and (2) when they promise by swearing what they do not intend to render, but they only do so in order to extract themselves by perjury from the present troubles by which they are held. Third, they sin who swear in trials when what they have sworn they do not render. It is concerning this point that the prophet says, "who swears to his neighbor and does not change." This kind of perjury was continually held to be notorious among the Gentiles. The ancient Romans were gifted with such integrity that they did not want to break a trust given by an oath even to their most intense enemies. The account of Attilius is noteworthy.[11] Now, indeed, the pontifical saying is that keeping faith is not for kings and magnates[12] but for merchants.

11. The reference concerns Marcus Regulus Attilius, a consular-general in the first Punic war and his ensuing captivity and death in approximately 248–250 BC. This is reportedly in Book 18 of *Livy's Ab Urbe Condita*, however, books 11–20 are lost. For a fourth-century AD Roman account, see Eutropius, *Breviarum ab urbe condite*, II.xx–xxv. For an account in English see Nathaniel Hooke's *The Roman History*, vol. 3, 4th ed. (Dublin: Watson, 1759), 155ff. Additionally, it is noteworthy that Niccolo Machiavelli, an older contemporary to Musculus, makes multiple references to this account in passing in *Discorsi sopra la prima deca di Tito Livio* (*Discourse upon the first ten books of T. Livy*). Machiavelli's work was published posthumously in 1531.

12. *magnatus* is a technical ecclesiastical term referring to archbishops, cardinals, and popes who, in this time period, are outside the jurisdiction of secular courts.

The Roman popes, after they had strengthened the covenants of kings and princes by taking an oath when it seemed advantageous to themselves, so many times broke them whenever they wished and released subordinates from an oath of fidelity by their own decrees (see Gratian's *Decretum*, Case 15, question 6). In such a way, Pope Nicholas absolved the bishop of Trier from the bonds of an oath.[13] In such a way, Pope Zachary deposed the king of the Franks and substituted Pepin, the father of Charlemagne, in his place and likewise absolved all those born Franks from an oath of fidelity.[14] Moreover, that temerity greatly displeases the Lord, as in the reign of Zedekiah when it was punished gravely when he treacherously severed his offered oath of fidelity to the king of Babylon (Ezra 17[:11–21). Fourth, those who swear are sinning when they swear and use the name of God in some illicit matter that they cannot carry out without sinning. In the case of a minster of the word, this happens if he should promise on oath that he refuses to censure the sins of a magnate or to speak against false doctrine. There are innumerable kinds of this sin. Therefore, when someone swears to offer a guarantee under the name of God, he should diligently foresee whether what he promises by an oath he can render without offense to God. Fifth, they sin in the form of the oath who join the names

---

13. Musculus is citing *Corpus Iuris Canonici*, Pars Secunda, Causa XV, Quaestio vi, caput 2. Pope Nicholas I (858–867) overruled the pact made between the archbishop John of Ravenna and the excommunicated archbishops Thietgaud of Trier and Günther of Cologne. See also *The Catholic Encyclopedia*, ed. C. G. Herbermann (New York: Encyclopedia Press, 1914), 11:54.

14. Musculus is citing *Corpus Iuris Canonici*, Pars Secunda, Causa XV, Quaestio 6, caput iii. The king of the Franks in question was Childeric III (Lat.: *Hildericus*), the last Merovingian king of the Franks who ruled from 743–752. Regarding the deposition of Childeric, see G. H. Pertzius and F. Kurze, *Annales Fuldenses sive Annales Regni Francorum Orientales ab Einhardo, Ruodolfo, Meginhardo Fuldensibus Seligenstadi, Fuldae, Mogontiaci Conscripti cum Continuationibus Ratisbonensi et Althahensibus* (Hannover: Bibliopoli Hahniani, 1891), 5–6.

of the saints to the name of God (concerning which kind of sin you recall from above). I wish to mention this concerning the abuse of oath-taking in a few words and in passing so that I may admonish pious persons for the purpose of learning in the case of oaths to take heed to themselves and to others, so that they may not consciously and knowingly sin in any way against the majesty of the divine name, being always mindful of that threat that he makes in the Decalogue, "For neither will God hold him guiltless whoever has used the name of the Lord his God in vain" [Ex. 20:7; Deut. 5:11].

## Concerning the Dissolution of Oaths

Because the prophet says, "whoever swears to his neighbor and does not change" [Ps. 15:4], it is not without cause that someone may ask whether there is not some reason for which an oath can be invalidated. Moreover, this question must be inspected, not on account of those who in general are held either by the least amount or not by any respect to an oath, but rather on account of those afflicted consciences who are compressed and constrained by the bonds of an oath in such a way that while they are compelled to keep the trust of the oath, they are confined to sin against God. Therefore, we must be consider those cases in which the bond of an oath must be broken.

First, the bond of an oath must be broken when an oath is illicit—that is, when both by swearing it and by keeping it one sins inasmuch as it is sworn to do what is contrary to the will of God. If a man in Israel dedicated a sacrifice to the idol Baal, that he might pass his son through the fire, or if he should dedicate to God the wages of a male prostitute[15] or of a whore, oaths of such kind were sworn illicitly and were also kept with great sin. If a married man should on oath renounce his own wife, it is

15. *precium canis:* lit. "wages of a dog." This is a Hebrew expression from Deuteronomy 23:18.

this same kind of great sin. Likewise, if someone dedicated an offering and worship to any of the saints, he sins by swearing and, to that point, sins more fully by keeping the oath.

Second, the bond of an oath must be broken when for the sake of keeping the oath a cause of sin is presented. Such kinds of oaths must be broken, or from this it must be proved wrong what is said in 22, question 4: "An oath is not instituted for this purpose so that it may be a bond of iniquity."[16] For example, the sacrificing priests, the monks, and the bishops are compelled to renounce legitimate marriage for the sake of preserving their celibacy. In order that this oath may be kept, they are not hindered from prostitution (indeed, they are only hindered from marriage and, therefore, the bond of their oath is not broken), and a cause for the miseries of many sins is presented. Such kinds of oaths are actually made not for righteousness and purity but for unrighteousness and impurity, and so frankly must be broken. For, with the apostle as a witness, "it is better to marry than to burn" [1 Cor. 7:9]. Nor was the apostle wishing to throw a noose upon believers, but he was allowing every one into this grace, which he had accepted freely from God and was not bound by any bond. The bishops ought to imitate the apostle's example, spirit, and doctrine if they were true bishops, and neither ought they to bind the consciences of the brethren to any bonds of an oath nor to retain them bound in a bond of iniquity for sinning but render them freely to God, who redeems them by his own blood from the snares of Satan. Indeed, because the church does not have such bishops but is subject to masters and princes, can any other counsel help the brethren than that, first, they should know that no oath ought to prevail with that reverence that it may be a bond of iniquity and of sins? Next, according to the apostle, if they can be made free, they should try and extract themselves from that snare of Satan and flee the tyranny of the

16. See the *Corpus Iuris Canonici*, Decreti Pars Secunda, Causa XXII, Quaestio iv, caput xxii.

bishops, so that, while they wish to keep their offered oath, they may not wrap themselves in the gravest sins and perish. Of such kind of sin is that account of Jephthah, who, because of his oath, sacrificed his very own daughter (Judg. [11:30–40]).[17] Herod wickedly slaughtered John the Baptist so that he might keep what he had sworn. Those men slaughtered these people against the will of God so that they might not perjure themselves. You brother, who continue in harlotry lest you should loosen your vow, you yourself are not slaughtering your body but, what is worse, your very own soul.

Third, an illicit oath must not be kept when, for the sake of it, someone sins against the love of his neighbor. If anyone might have sworn for the murder of his neighbor, the oath must be dissolved. For the example of David, see 1 Samuel 25[:1–35]. You should learn today that those who would swear on oath that they would give to no one absolutely, or give so small an amount in return, are once and again deceived. In this oath, they guard themselves so that they may not help the needs of their brethren. Such kinds of oaths fight with the love of neighbor and are opposed to the doctrine of Christ. Therefore, they cannot be kept without sin. Those who spend any time in monasteries are bound in such a way by the bond of a monastic vow that they cannot expend themselves even for the duties of humanity, much less the obligations of children (not to mention Christian love for parents, brothers, sisters, and other Christians), and they cannot please the Lord. Therefore, those oaths must be dissolved so that, because someone is a captive of human establishments, one may be free to be placed under the yoke of Christ. Thus, the apostle says, "You have been bought with a great price, do not desire to be made slaves of men" (1 Cor. 7[:23]).

Fourth, an oath or a vow does not prevail upon those who are not subject to their own right but are subject to the power of another. Therefore, because those have sworn completely without

17. Musculus cites this as Judges 2.

their own consent, the oath cannot lawfully be kept, even if they vowed something to the Lord God. The clearest argument for this matter is from what is written in Numbers 30[:2–5] in this way:

> This is the speech that the Lord commanded: If any of the men vowed a vow to the Lord or constrained himself by an oath, he will not make void his word, but he will fulfill all that he promised. If a woman, who is in her father's house and still in the age of her maidenhood should vow something and constrain herself by an oath, if her father should become cognizant of the vow that has been promised and the oath by which she obligated her own soul and he shall remain silent, she will be liable to the vow. Whatever she has promised and vowed, she will fulfill the work. If, however, when he heard it, the father should contradict it, both her vow and her oath will be void nor will she be held liable to the promise, because her father contradicted it.

In a similar fashion also it is subjoined concerning wives, so that the vows and oaths of wives are plainly void if, when the husbands should hear of it, he contradicts it. From this, it is clearly handed down that promises and vows of this sort that have been made by those who are not subject to their own right, unless the consent of those to whose power they are subject is added, must not be kept but must be dissolved as void. Therefore, it ought not to be supposed valid if either a son or a daughter, in contradicting their parents, binds themselves in marriage; the power of this matter belongs to the father (see 1 Cor. 7[:36–38]), which ought not to be annulled. Next, it is also plainly iniquity if a son or daughter, in resisting and contradicting his or her parents, casts off his or her father's power and enters into a monastery and is there subject to the unknown authority of some monk or nun. Therefore, it is absolutely impious and against the divine law, whoever the author of the act may be, that children would be hurried into trampling over their parents in the threshold by the monastic superstition. Thus that saying of Christ is fulfilled:

"You make void the commandment of God on account of your own inventions. For God said, 'Honor your mother and father,' and, 'Whoever will curse his father or mother, let him be put to death'" (Matt. 15[:4–6]). Moreover, such are those who teach that parents also must be trampled upon and trod underfoot if they should stand in the way, and thus the children must fly away to the monastery. Who does not see how much lighter and tolerable it was when the scribes and Pharisees were teaching that it might be said to parents that "the services I offer to the temple also profit you" [Matt. 15:5]? First, they were teaching them to offer gifts to the temple of God. Next, they were admonishing them how they might satisfy parents by the explanation and meaning of the temple gifts. In so doing, the authors were indeed diminishing the help owed to parents, yet, meanwhile, they were not teaching sons to withdraw themselves entirely from the power of their parents nor were they commanding that parents should be trampled upon in their doors. Yet, the Lord dashes them upon the broad commandment of God concerning honoring parents that they rendered void by their own inventions. I beseech you, do we think that the Lord is in this way not immutable, so that he may suspend or change his way of thinking against those authors who have sinned more gravely and immensely?

Fifth, an oath offered concerning an impossible thing does not bind. Moreover, I call a thing impossible, not only when it is in itself impossible, but also when it is impossible for the one swearing and vowing. As an example, to lead an angelic life is a thing in itself quite possible, but for angels, not for humans as humans. To keep the continence of virginity even if possible for those who have received this gift from God, is nevertheless not possible for everyone. "Whoever can take hold of this, let him take it," says Christ [Matt. 19:12]. Therefore, if it should be impossible for him who has sworn to lead an angelic life as he has been constituted in the flesh, it is more preferable that he rescind his stupid and ill-advised promise than continue confined in a bond of an impossible thing, falling into a life no longer human but devilish. Paul did not want widows under sixty years old to be supported by the subsidy of the church [1 Tim. 5:9–14], but today boys and girls are compelled to keep a vow of celibacy when they have no experience as to whether they might have received the gift of virginal continence from the Lord. Therefore, counsel should be given to all who on account of the impossibility of this thing will fall apart to vices of libidinous flesh and a roving filthiness, so that recovering their senses from this stupid vow, they may flee to the counsel of the apostle who says: "On account of shunning harlotry, let each man have his own wife and each woman have her own husband" (1 Cor. 7[:2]). This case, because it concerns the loosening of vows and oaths, could be treated in multiple and broad ways. Indeed, I think these things abundantly suffice for noncontentious persons.

# Concerning Usury*

Among the remaining evils of this present age, the plague of usury has also continuously grown up, and has become ripe for divine vengeance, so that I may clearly testify that whatever I say on this topic—although I should say it with much earnestness and even with a singular zeal—is in vain. This, accordingly, we have been acquainted with by experience—namely, that this evil, moreover, was only acknowledged by the majority of men when in our age it began to be brought forward and rebuked openly in the opinions and writings of pious and learned men. It is almost like having a surgery on a cancer only in its destructive stage rather than previously in its growing stage. This surgery occurs only after a just and fitting diagnosis that the cancer is

* This treatise is the second of two appendices to the commentary on Psalm 15. This translation is based on Wolfgang Musculus, *In Davidis Psalterium sacrosanctum Commentarij: In quibus et reliqua catholicae religionis nostrae Capita passim, non praetermissis orthodoxorum etiam Patrum sententijs, ita tractantur, ut Christianus lector nihil desiderare amplius possit* (Basel: Herwagen, 1573), 1137–46.

now entirely destructive and incurable. Therefore, it would not be without cause that I consider this undertaking a vain work, and, as the proverb goes, "I appear to wash a brick," were I not constrained by the bond of a promise and yielding to the will of the brethren. For this reason, I am speaking about usury, insofar as it might be conducive for pious persons and those not yet hopelessly seized by this pestilential disease. I know that when it has been debated, even by those learned and pious men, concerning usury, it is not argued in the German manner but, actually, in the manner of the schools of foreign nations. To be sure, the scholastic decisions are no less complex than the intricate nature of this sort of avarice, but I will by no means touch upon that topic, but, rather, I will simply mention those things that, it seems to me, must be said without any sort of thorny debate. To that end, in the first place, I will say what usury is. Next, in order to see whether it is lawful for Christians, I will compare that practice with the teaching of Christ and with the profession of the Christian religion.

## What Usury Is

Lest anyone should call me one of those who defend usury as a right, I will produce a definition of usury that I have not devised but has been advanced previously in several ages by those whose piety has obtained more authority in the church of Christ than can be uprooted by the usurers or their patrons. Jerome writes in his sixth book on Ezekiel in this way: "Indeed, some think that usury is only upon money, which divine Scripture foresees as the theft of the superabundance of everything, so that you may not take back more than you have given."[1] Likewise, others customarily accept a small interest of various kinds for borrowed

1. See S. *Eusebii Hieronymi Stridonensis Commentariorum in Ezechielem Prophetam Libri Quatuordecim* in J. P. Migne's *Patrologia Latina* (Paris: Garnier Fratres, 1884), 25:176C. In this passage, Jerome is commenting on Ezekiel 18:8.

money, and they do not realize that Scripture also calls interest a superabundance, whatever it may be, which they have received from what they have given. This is what Ambrose says in *On Naboth*:[2]

> The majority of those fleeing the commandment of the law, when they have given money to wholesale traders, do not exact usury on the money, but they gain from their merchandise just as if they gained from the benefits of usury. For this reason, let us hear what the law says: "Neither," it says, "will you accept usury on food, nor on all other things." Therefore on food, it is usury; on clothes it is usury; and whatever approaches capital that bears interest, as well as whatever other name you wish to give it, is usury.

Augustine, on Psalm 36, defines usury also in this way: "If you lend to a person, that is, you give your money for a return, from which you expect to receive more than you have given, not the money only, but anything more than you gave, whether that may be wheat or wine or oil or whatever it is—if you expect to receive more than you gave, you are a money-lender and in this must be condemned."[3] Therefore, according to the opinion of these, usury is not only the reception, but also the hope and expectation for something beyond your principal, as they say: "This is beyond what has been given, in whatever name it may at last be disguised. For a change of the name does not destroy the malice of the remaining vice." Ezekiel 18[:8, 13, 17] sufficiently proves its guilt. Usury is what is received beyond one's principal, when the prophet says, "you will not give for usury, and you will not take the superabundance." For as David Kimhi rightly exposits: "What it is to give for usury is exposited by the following clause, when it is added, 'and he will not accept

2. Actually a citation of Ambrose's treatise against usury, *On Tobias*. See *S. Ambrosii Mediolanensis Episcopi De Tobia Liber Unus* in *Patrologia Latina*, 14:778B–C.

3. See *Nicene and Post-Nicene Fathers*, 1st series, 8:99.

a superabundance.'"[4] Also Leviticus 25:[36–37] reads in the following manner: "You will not take from him usury and a superabundance, but you will fear your God. You will not give your gold to him for usury, and you will not give your food so that you may receive a superabundance." Also Caesar's Laws in the Codex concerning usury in a similar way call usury what is received beyond one's principal.[5] Yet, they permit the use of it in a certain way, concerning which we will afterward speak. Additionally, the Latins have called usury what is received for the use of the money as though it were some sort of compensation, where one returns to the lender some benefit. The Greeks call it τόκον, so to speak, as a certain gain from a monetary principal. In Hebrew, it is called נשך from "stinging," because ultimately it stings whoever pays the usury. Up to this point I have spoken concerning what usury is.

## Whether Usury Is Lawful?

Here we are not inquiring about usury upon usury (*usura usurarum*), which the Jews employ, which no one hesitates to call unlawful and detestable (nor in any way should it be endured), but rather about simple usury, in which more is received than what is given, whether it is much or little and whether it is prac-

4. Rabbi David Kimhi (1160–1235), also known as רדק, was a prolific and proficient biblical commentator, philosopher, and Hebrew grammarian. For a relatively accessible translation including Kimhi's comments on Psalm 15, see *The Longer Commentary of R. David Kimhi on the First Book of Psalms (I–X, XV–XVII, XIX, XXII, XXIV)*, trans. by R. G. Finch (London: SPCK, 1919), 69–73. For editions published within Musculus' lifetime, see *Tehilim Mishle p'Kav ve-naki* (Saloniki: Joseph ben Abraham Hayyun, 1522); and *Sefer Tehilim 'im perush Rabi David Kimhi* (Iznah: Paul Fagius, 1542).

5. For the Latin text, see *Corpus Iuris Civilis*, vol. 2, ed. Paulus Kreuger, 11th ed. (Berolini: Weidmannsche Verlagsbuchhandlung, 1954), *Codex* IV.xxxii.26, secs. 1–5, p. 173. For an English translation of the *Codex*, see *The Code of Justinian*, trans. Samuel P. Scott (Cincinnati: 1932), IV.xxxii.26, secs. 1–5.

ticed with money or other things. Some think this is not unlawful in itself, unless it becomes illicit through illicit circumstances. I do not deny that there is a kind of usury that can be found that is not only lawful, but also useful. This is the sort of usury that they call *erd vucher*—that is, a usury of the ground through which much more is received than has been committed to the earth by the sowing of seed. The one who gives everything to everyone renders this usury and yet does not have less as a result. That usury is given in such a way to the recipients that no harm is given and conveys the most benefit; and, yet, God forbid that it would be condemned as avarice or, even more, that it would be preached against on account of a manifest benevolence and very clear beneficence! Look! Here is a lawful, useful, and divine interest for you through which Abraham and Isaac became wealthy. Through this means at one time thirtyfold, at another time sixtyfold, and at another time even a hundredfold—and it is given without sin by God, and it is received by man. At one time, this kind of interest was most studiously protected by our ancestors, which is now considered even worthless, and is confined to the monetarily criminal. There is also another kind of interest through which it is lawful to receive back a hundred for one without sin. Christ personally promises this kind to his own believers as a guarantor in the place of his Father, saying: "And everyone who leaves behind a house, or brothers, or sisters, or father, or mother, or wife, or children, or fields on account of my name will receive a hundredfold, and will possess eternal life" (Matt. 19[:29]). See, this other, heavenly kind of interest to which we are also called is so lacking in us that we may be frightened away by it. How few, I pray, are there who cast their souls to collect heavenly wealth with such interest?

From these examples of interest, it is at least established that by itself it is not unlawful to render more than you receive or even to receive more than you gave. Indeed, it should be that the same reason for this sort of usury that prevails in our era and concerning which we presently ask—which is either earthly or heavenly, according to which God himself is the greatest lender of all—at last must be considered by simple and pure eyes. Whoever defends customary usury devises many things to protect it and from which they assert that it is not unlawful. They bring forward the law from the Codex in the treatment concerning usury, in which one percent, a half percent, and other such things are permitted—no, more correctly—established, and they think it is done by the authority of civil law so that what they do is either not usury or, if it is usury, it is not unlawful usury. We respond that the legislator was compelled by necessity, not so that he might protect usury, but so that he might impose some rule upon the increasing avarice, which the text of the law itself demonstrates. For it raises the gravity and enormity of usury as a crime, and prescribes certain methods beyond which nothing may be asked. It is by far doubtful that a law to preserve charity should be wished for among Christians in order that there may be no place for usury. Indeed, because avarice used to thrive to such an enormous extent, he judged it necessary that by a certain predetermined rate it should be hindered as if by a barrier, and in that way he cut back at every point the enormity of usury to half of its previous size. Therefore, it is so far removed from the fact that the law is protecting usury and renders it illicit so that it bears more witness to the fact that charity has grown cold among Christians and that the most base and detestable avarice has burst forth continuously to the point that, in order to restrain it, the imperial authority was necessary. Just as when Moses brought forth the law for the repudiation and divorce of a wife, it was not excusing the Jew before God, who employed it so that divorce may not be liable to wound marriage [Deut. 24:1–3]. Likewise, the civil law did not make usury lawful so that a Christian, by using it, may be rendered guiltless before God. Hence, in the same way Christ spoke to the Jews about the law of divorce: "From the beginning it was not so," and "on account of the hardness of your heart Moses permitted to you a certificate of divorce" [Matt. 19:3–8]. In this way, he sent them back to the commencement of legitimate marriage to which they ought to conform themselves. We also must consider the purity, first principles, righteousness, and justice (משפח) of the Christian religion in this case of usury. Concerning usury, therefore, one should look at Matthew 5[:42] and Luke 6[:30–36] and not civil laws. For civil laws are not produced on account of Christians, for whom there is no need for a civil law about this to restrain them in their zeal for avarice, lest they leap across the rule. Christians are led by the Spirit in such a way that they love their neighbor from their heart and would provide not only their money for their neighbor if it should be necessary, but they would also expend their very life for their neighbor. When that kind of love prevails, there is no place for any striving after avarice, nor is there a reason that laws of this sort should be fixed by which a method of avarice is established. Therefore, the intent of the legislator was not so that he might protect someone who demands usury in return for lending money, but so that he might look out for the one taking the loan, lest, since that person is pressed by a necessity, he should be compelled to take money by a loan (because charity has grown cold he does not find anyone who freely and without usury will give him a loan), and would be plundered through the unquenchable avarice of the usurers. Therefore, that law given by the Christian emperor concerning usury contains the argument in which, to the shame of the Christian name, it is proven that the love of neighbor has grown cold. It is so far from the point that he absolves usury so that it is now lawful. Christians, on one hand, are led internally by the Holy Spirit and, on the other hand, are called away from all those things that displease God by the light and authority of the word of God so that the constraint of the imperial law is not necessary either to compel or to deter them. Civil laws do not forbid all things that are illicit before God, and, besides, those things that they do not forbid they also do not punish. For that reason, it does not follow that all those things that are not forbidden by civil laws are lawful before God. Civil laws do not prohibit wrath, indignation, impatience, envy, hatred, pride, evil concupiscence, avarice, and whatever other things of this sort that the apostle calls the works of the flesh (Gal. 5[:19–21]) and things that exclude those who are so inclined from the kingdom of God. Therefore, for this reason no one doing such things is excused in the sight of God simply because it is not condemned by any civil law. Conversely, civil laws do not command all those things that are required for true justice. No civil law prescribes faith, hope, and love for God and neighbor, patience in adversity, kindness, gentleness, humility and modesty, and other such things. Yet, no one ought to think that they are not held to those things for the reason that he is not condemned by any civil law if he has been motivated by a disposition contrary to those things. In addition, to some extent they permit with certain reasons those things that are nevertheless unlawful before God and are condemned by his word. Moreover, they permit not only things right and lawful in themselves, but also exclude those things which are rather wicked. Thus, civil laws also permit usury to a certain extent so that a rule for avarice is laid down. They do not punish fornication;[6] they do not destroy brothels. No one excuses a fornicator before God, nor is what the apostle says in Hebrews 13[:4] rendered void: "Marriage is honorable and sacred, moreover, the Lord will judge fornicators and adulterers." In a similar manner, all those threats that condemn usurers in the Holy Scriptures are not rendered void because they are not condemned by the civil laws. Rather, the goal of the civil law must be considered. Nor must it be supposed that civil laws have been produced so that they may render people just before God, but rather that they may make the state of human society in some way at all times tolerable and may put down human malice. I have wished to

6. *scortatatio*: lit. "whoring," including all the aspects—client, prostitute, and pimp—as well as the general category of premarital and extramarital sexual practices; thus, fornication. A *scortator* can be a prostitute, a pimp, a client, or a fornicator.

touch upon these things so that I may respond to those who defend the usury of our times under the pretext of civil law in such a way that they deny that usury is unlawful before God.

## How a Loan Ought to Be Given According to the Teaching of Christ

Because we are inquiring in this place about usury, whether it is lawful or unlawful, not before the world, but before God, the pretext of civil law and whatever sort of human arrangement may exist cannot have a place in this question. The rationale of a Christian profession constrains us that we should listen to Christ, the very Son of God, and that we should learn from his mouth how Christians ought to lend in such a way that they do not sin in the sight of the Lord. It is suitable to convince us that whatever struggles against the doctrine of our Savior cannot be lawfully practiced. Therefore, we must consider what kind of usury is consistent with the words of Christ. Moreover, I assert first and foremost that I do not speak to the children of this age but to believing persons who have been convinced that the teaching of Christ is divine and contains the norm of true piety and righteousness, so that all those who do not adapt themselves to it, from their heart, necessarily displease God.

We read in Matthew 5[:42]: "You may not deny someone wishing to take a loan from you." Luke 6[:34–35]: "Give a loan, hoping nothing from it. Even if you should give a loan from which you hope to receive something, what credit is that to you? For even sinners give a loan to sinners so that they may receive a settlement of a debt." With these words, Christ has established how Christians ought to conduct themselves in this case. Additionally, he distinguishes between believers and the sons of this age. First, he commands that they may not deny those wishing to take a loan. Understand that this is only if someone has the means to give a loan. If someone does not have the money himself, how could he give a loan to another person? He does not permit his own people who have the substance of this world the freedom to give or not to give. In other words, this shows that whoever refuses to give a loan to needy persons asking for a loan is a stranger to the kingdom of God and that true justice is a mark of the sons of God. Thus, he admonishes his own that they may not do that, if it pertains to them and they wish to be numbered among the sons of God. The sons of this age do not acknowledge this commandment nor are they bound to it by civil laws, but they wish to be free to give a loan or not to give a loan. Nor do they believe that they sin if they deny someone who asks, when they are able to help someone. Therefore, if someone is pleased to profess the Christian religion, he must take care that he is motivated differently than the sons of this age. It is more than enough of a sin insofar as we deny our wealth to a person wanting to receive a loan. It is in fact excessive because, just as if we were unbelievers, we do not believe it to be sin for us not to discharge the duty of charity to a brother seeking a loan, as if those things that Christ says are trivial: "You may not deny a person wanting to receive a loan from you." Some say that those things are not commanded, but it is expressly commanded in the Jewish counsels in Deuteronomy 15[:7–8] in this rule: "If one of your brethren who dwells within the gates of your city in the land which the Lord your God will give to you should come to poverty, you will not harden your heart, nor will you draw back your hand but you will open it to a poor man, and you will give a loan to him whom you notice in need." Therefore, how is it fitting that the justice of the law of Moses is more complete than the gospel of Christ? Are we free to perform or omit a work of charity that even the Jews were not free to do?

Even if the counsel in that passage would have said, "you may not refuse a person wanting to take a loan from you," in what way is it appropriate for Christians to turn Christ's counsel, which has been set forth so earnestly, upside down and to think that it can be condemned with impunity? Moreover he says, "I say to you who hear" [Luke 6:27]. Therefore, whoever wants to be hearers of Christ are held to the obedience of this counsel, and they cannot turn their back on it without sin and detriment to their own salvation, just as the sick cannot neglect the counsels of a doctor without damage to their health. Indeed, Deuteronomy 15[:9] is clear that whoever refuses a loan to a brother seeking a loan sins against the will of God. "Let him not cry out against you to the LORD," he says, "and it be done to you according to your sin."

Additionally, Christ prescribes to his own how they ought to give a loan. "Give a loan," he says, "hoping for nothing from it" [Luke 6:35]. Some think in this way that no advantage, no gain, or no profit beyond that which is given in the loan must be hoped for and received—namely, that this is what indeed is required from him who desires to keep his hand back entirely from the impurity of usury. Indeed, that does not do justice to the intention of Christ, who demands from us in this place that we should give a loan to those from whom we can hope to receive back nothing. It is sufficiently clear from those things, which he attached, when he says, "If you should give a loan which you hope to receive back, what credit is that to you? For even sinners give a loan to sinners so that they may receive a settlement" [Luke 6:34]. He does not say, "so that they may receive usury, a superabundance, something beyond the sum given as a loan," but "so that they may receive a settlement." Therefore, Christ also distinguishes here between his own and the rest who are not his. He requires from his own that they help their neighbor and brother not only without reference to their own advantage when they make the loan to someone and sinners, but also without reference to their own loss and the expense of the money given as a loan. In this manner, they are to give the loan so that they procure credit for themselves from God. This also must be distinguished between the Gentiles and the Christians. The Gentiles give a loan (1) to the sort who can make good on whatever they received, (2) to those who gave or can give a loan to someone and to themselves, (3) to friends and relatives, and (4) to those from whom they can hope for some credit. For in these kinds of giving there is no sin. To be sure, however, the justice of the spirit of Christ and of his kingdom are not yet expressed. Therefore, whoever are Christ's give a loan as follows: (1) to those who do not have hardly the means to be able to make good on the loan, (2) to those who neither ever gave a loan to anyone nor could give a loan in return, (3) not only to friends, but also to enemies, and not only to relations, but also to strangers and foreigners, and (4) when there is even no thanks given and still less can thanks be hoped for in some way. As long as they do those things, they declare again that they themselves are sons of the one who makes the sun to shine upon the good and the evil and the rain to fall upon the grateful and the ungrateful. Christ also demands it from his own "so that you may be sons of your Father" [Luke 6:35].

Compare also those who give a loan for usury to this norm of Christian righteousness, and see how far removed it is from the standard of Christ's words, which have been set forward nevertheless to all Christians, so that unless they conform themselves to it, they ought to be counted among sinners, not among the children of God—no indeed, they do not even possess the righteousness of sinners! Enough righteousness is attributed even to sinners that they may give a loan without usury and desire to receive no gain in its place, but only what they should give as a loan. Even from this, by comparison with ourselves, who consider the righteousness of the kingdom of Christ, the precept of the words of Christ, and the profession of the Christian religion, it is most easy to give a judgment about usury—namely, that it is unlawful for those who ascribe their name to Christ and wish to appear as Christians. Concerning unbelievers, we may not judge. A Christian is responsible to answer for his own profession, neither to judge about things—whether they may be lawful or unlawful—differently than it is ordered according to the teaching of Christ, nor to set his own boundary in the pursuit of justice by which he can escape the guilt of injustice in a secular court, but rather the boundary is set where he can escape the guilt of injustice in the sight of God. Therefore, we likewise conclude with the Holy Scriptures and the words of Christ that usury—which in a remarkable way at last in this era grows up even in the church of Christ—is not lawful, but rather that it is damnable and most foreign to a profession of Christian justice.

Indeed, how great is the iniquity of usury considered in itself! It is not truly difficult to learn, except by those for whom the stench of profit is sweet in whatever way they have concocted the matter, whose minds have been blinded by the pursuit of avarice. First, the vice of avarice is the basest disposition not only among Christians, but even among the Gentiles. That is the root of usury. Remove this love of money (φιλαργυρίαν) together with covetousness (πλεονεξίᾳ), and we will not have usurers in the church of Christ.

Second, who does not see how unjust it is to run after the gain from another's work and hard-earned savings? In fact, the usury, which is given not from a usurer, but the usury of the one paying, comes about only by his worry and concern.

Third, it is also foreign to equity, because the usurer without any expense of his own money and without risk receives a profit, so that he is not liable for any loss however the dice fall; rather, only the poor wretch who pays the usury is compelled to endure the cost of a misfortune. The whole of this matter concerns what loss occurs. Indeed, nothing concerns the moneylender except that the profit from the principal is received intact.

Fourth, it also must be added that however much usury there is, and although the debtor should pay for many years without any interruption, yet the greatest part of the principal remains untouched, nor is any of it worn away. Moreover, those things torture the soul of the one paying usury and diminish his resources. There is no need to admonish against it when that is the well-known experience. When there is someone of this sort, experiencing this inescapable plague by means of a dejected soul, he forsakes his wife and children, and what is left of his resources he relinquishes to the insatiable avarice of the moneylender who is taking possession of them. We read that that kind of thing overthrew those who, oppressed by foreign money, took themselves to David who was in exile (1 Sam. 22[:2]). The pious daily see spectacles of this sort right before their very eyes with sorrow and a sigh, while magistrates turn a blind eye. Meanwhile—what is the most oppressive of all—when these sorts of moneylenders ought not even to have a place in a state, they nevertheless acquire ecclesiastical as well as civil offices.

## But the Moneylender Objects

"It is a well-known saying," he says, "in everyone's mouth, that I do not want to do injury. I do not cause anyone to come; I compel no one to take money from me. Besides, money is sold and received from me by nothing other than a condition of usury, nor is anything else asked for. How do I sin in this matter? Let my money remain with me if the damage of usury is so great." I respond: Those sentiments are not those of a Christian person, but plainly of a Gentile—nay, more correctly—of an inhuman person. Compelled by that cruel spur of necessity, those people come to you as wretches, and you, who are without any sense of humanity for their misery, you most shamefully render them lucrative for yourself.

Again the moneylender objects: "Notwithstanding, when they take money from me under the condition of usury, they rejoiced and even gave thanks. Finally, what kind of injury is this that produces joy and goodwill?" I respond: Because the wretches are rejoicing and giving thanks, it is not from the fact that they perceive it as a benefit, but because, with their need spurring them, they think that by the cost of usury they can avert being presently overwhelmed by their necessity. By all means, they would prefer money simply in a loan than to accept along with it the cost of usury. Indeed, because such inhumanity prevails that they should find no kindness anywhere, they certainly rejoice over money received by usury, but this kind of joy in the end degenerates into the greatest woe. While it seems to them that they have avoided Charybdis on one side, they fall into Scylla on the other.

Chrysostom most helpfully compares the joy of those that receive money subject to usury to the bite of an asp[7]—that is, in the way that someone is stricken by the bite of an asp as though he were lying down in a pleasant sleep and dies by the sweetness of a lethal and deep sleep, in which the venom progresses through all his members during his sleep. Likewise, whoever accepts money by usury in this way certainly rejoices at the time of the loan as if the moneylender is moved by kindness. Yet, the usury races through all his resources, converting the whole of them into debt.[8] When Cato the Elder was asked what it is to lend money at usury, he responded that it is the very same thing as to kill someone.[9]

Third, those who especially have some experience in appearing to exhibit the gospel of Christ, not by which they correct themselves, but by which they disguise their own wickedness, retort: "Notwithstanding, the whole summary of the law and

7. This is a common citation in the Western exegetical tradition of Christianity from the patristic period through the Reformation when commenting upon Matthew 5:20. For example, this citation of Chrysostom can be found in Thomas Aquinas's *Catena Aurea in quatuor Evangelia Expositio Matthaeum*, Lectio 20. The Latin and Greek text of Chrysostom is also available in Migne's *Patrologia Graeca* (Paris: Migne, 1859), 56:701, which attributes this quote to Pseudo-Chrysostom by its inclusion in the *Opus imperfectum in Matthaeum*.

8. Musculus employs a clever and subtle pun on the word *facultates*, which can mean either "faculties" or "resources." On one hand, the poison of an asp dulls one's faculties coursing (*cursus*) through their veins, meaning their bodily faculties; likewise, interest poisons all of one's financial faculties or resources, racing (*cursus*) through their assets.

9. This is reported by M. Tullius Cicero in *De Officiis*, variously called *Of Duties* or *Of Offices*. For the Latin text and English translation, see the Loeb Classical Library Edition, *De Officiis*, trans. Walter Miller (Cambridge: Harvard University Press, 1938), bk. II.25, 265–67.

the prophetic Scriptures, as Christ himself witnesses, is well-known—namely, that whatever I desire done to me, likewise I may also do to others [Matt. 7:12; Luke 6:31]. I would not choose even for myself any other condition than that for one hundred florins I will repay five florins every year. Therefore, what sin is committed in this because I receive the equivalent from others? I employ the same condition as often as it is necessary. I give the equivalent to others, and, in return, I take the equivalent from others." I respond: This is a most unjust abuse of the words of Christ, which have been set forth not to protect avarice, but rather brotherly charity. Of course, you do the same thing to others that you ask from others! If, however, you did this out of a spirit of charity, then put yourself in the place of a poor and destitute person, and put on the condition of that necessity, thinking what you wish to be done to you by those who are wealthy if you were in their place? Would you prefer that they give you a loan with usury or without usury? I doubt by far that you would prefer the one with usury. For a loan without usury would be more advantageous to your own affairs than if you would endure the cost of usury. Therefore, when Christ says, "what you wish done to you, do this also to others," you ought to understand that this is to say: "If you were in the situation that your neighbor is in, whatever you wish were done to you, you should do to those as a friend with the disposition of goodwill and benevolence, with which you are animated toward yourself." Examine your own conscience and judge with equity whether you would speak truly that you have loved and helped your poor and destitute neighbor in such a way that you wish others would love and help you, just as if you were situated in the same place. How can you when you cannot truly profess about yourself that what is kept by deceit mocks Christ our Savior's meaning? Next, you personally give usury to others and you receive it from others. I understand that, but I implore you, tell me, from what motive do you give usury? By what necessity? Are those things given to the person from whom you receive usury? No indeed! Destitute people undergo usury because of a disadvantage compelled by necessity. On the other hand, you undergo it not as a disadvantage but from the hope of greater profit, not by necessity, but with the disposition of avarice. You give five percent, so that you may receive ten, fifteen, or twenty. Thus, in this position, you give and you take usury, just as they were accustomed to do for a sacrificing priest, offering to the priest an *obol*[10] at the altars so that the priests may retain the gain of the offering in the church. By their own example, they call for the common people to offer it, and for this reason for one little piece of money, they steal ten. Thus simony most beautifully harmonizes with usury. Obviously, both are produced from the same spirit of avarice!

Fourth, when a moneylender senses that he is hemmed in and does not see by what rationale he can protect his usury, he flips to other wiles and says, "If the cause of usury is considered in this way so that I should sin by receiving it, I know what I will do. I will not give a loan from my money to anyone. I will save it for myself, lest I should be a usurer." I respond: This is the flight of avarice, in which regard the laws of the emperor do not wish to prohibit usury in its entirety. Do you wish to save your money? Before a secular court it is lawful, but, on the contrary, in Christ's court, by whose commandment you are bound, you may not deny one wanting to take a loan from you, and you should give a loan hoping to receive nothing in return. Therefore, whatever you do, you declare that you are nothing but less than a Christian, whether you should refuse to give a loan to a brother seeking one when you are able, or you should give a loan in such a way that you take usury. In either case, you sin both against Christ and against your neighbor. At least you do not preserve the vice of usury if you give absolutely no loans, yet you still cherish the true root of usury—avarice, of course—in your heart and you are a transgressor of Christ's word. If you give a loan for usury, again you sin against the command of Christ. In

10. An *obol* is a Greek coin equal to ⅙ of a drachma.

summary, much is against you! You equally ruin your neighbor by not only giving him a loan but also by giving him a loan for usury. If you should refuse to give a loan, you are worse than a Gentile sinner. Even sinners give a loan to sinners so that they may receive a settlement [Luke 6:34]. If you give with an eye to usury, even in that way you are worse than countless Gentiles, who avoid this vice by the law of nature.

Fifth, the avarice of a moneylender also retorts in this way: "If I should give a loan without usury, it will occur that what is mine might not be restored to me, for the poor man does not have such resources to render the whole sum. Indeed, if he should give a certain amount of usury in a single year, at least some amount of my money is restored to me." I respond: Well then, you recognize that your brother is so poor that he cannot repay the money given as a loan? Why, then, do you not yield to the words of Christ in Luke 6[:35] where he says, "and your reward will be much in heaven and you will be sons of the Most High," and in Luke 14[:14], "and will it not be repaid to you in the regeneration of the just?" How is it you receive nothing when an eternal benefit is the return on an earthly one? Consequently, that pretext is absolutely contrary to the doctrine of Christ, who on account of this very cause teaches us to do good to a poor man because he does not have the resources from which he may repay; for that reason one can acquire a heavenly reward. You, on account of that very fact that he is poor, do not wish to give a loan because he does not have the resources to restore to you what he takes from you. Therefore, either you do not believe that what Christ promises is true, or you are influenced more by temporary profit than by an eternal one, by an earthly profit more than a heavenly one.

Sixth, he says, "What I have, I amassed with great care and solicitude. By what rationale should I loan it to others for nothing? What is it to me that others do not look after their own affairs in the same way that I do? What do I owe to them?" I respond: Does this measure up at all to Christ, who redeemed you with his own blood on the cross and for your sake became a poor person, so that he might make you a wealthy one [2 Cor. 8:9]? Next, is it holding fast to Christ when we do not pay better attention to our salvation? In regard to what you owe to your brother, hear the apostle: "You are not to owe anything to anyone except that you mutually love one another" (Rom. 13[:8]). Therefore, you owe love to a needy brother and, for this reason, not merely your own money. Why? Because as Christ loved and gave himself for us, "we ought also to lay down our very souls for our brothers" (1 John 3[:16]). We all fail most in this matter because, short of the disposition of true love, we consider the poverty and humiliation of our brethren and not the greater will of God and his clear commandment (I will pass over in silence that immense esteem of his gratuitous redemption). Do you think a poor person is unworthy to receive your free gift? Christ is not unworthy who requires this from you. Do you think a poor person undeserving of such a kindness? Christ deserves it. Do you think a poor person cannot make good on what he takes? Christ can make good a hundredfold and likewise can give everlasting life just as he promised in Matthew 19[:29].

Seventh, as avarice is the most pertinacious of all idlers, a usurer still objects, saying, "By what means will I live? By what means will I take care of myself and my family, if a loan must be given in such a way that I do not receive anything back?" I respond: It has been said by the Lord: "Seek first the kingdom of God and his justice, and all these things will be added to you," and "all these things the Gentiles seek" [Matt. 6:32–33]. Therefore, this turning our backs on someone is not for Christians, nor is this fearful attitude, lest we should wrongly look out for our own things in helping our destitute brothers. In Proverbs 11[:24–25], we read as follows: "Some distribute their own things and are made richer still, others seize what is not their own and are always in want. The soul that blesses"—that is, does well—"will be made fat; and whoever may make drunk, he himself also will be made drunk." In Isaiah 58[:7–11], "Break your bread for the hungry," he says, "and bring the destitute and wandering into your home. When you should see the naked cover him, and you should not despise your own flesh. When you will stretch out your soul to the hungering and you will rebuild the afflicted soul, you will be like a well-watered garden, and like a spring of water, whose water will not run short." The apostle in 2 Corinthians 9[:9] says, "Scatter, give to the poor, and his righteousness remains forever. He bestows seed for sowing and will offer his bread for the chewing." Therefore, a faithful man must not fear penury because he helps the poor. Yet, I do not wish to pass judgment, as long as that passage of the apostle prevails that "the abundance of the wealthy should succor a brother's poverty" (2 Cor. 8[:14]). If the necessities are not communicated to others rather promptly, it could be tolerated, but it should not be excused. Rather, the weakness of faith should be recognized. Indeed, who will approve of this in the church of Christ, that poverty is not dreaded in such luxury of things? Indeed, is it dreaded when a brother must be helped with necessities? If we would follow the apostolic rule, which is prescribed in 1 Timothy [6:8] in this way, "having what we need to eat and what we need to be clothed, we are content," there is little place for that alarm. "For nature," as the proverb says, "with a little is dismissed, but gluttony certainly desires an immense amount." What is honest may be worked for, haste may be avoided, luxury may be abandoned, an abuse of all things eliminated, and we will be secure under the protection and the providence of God, nor will there be a need to dread the inevitability of penury. When so many costs are devoted to superb and splendid buildings, luxurious clothes, and all kinds of esculent delights—I pass over in silence the innumerable remainder of unnecessary things—is it any marvel that poverty is dreaded if the gain of usury is not abandoned? One who lavishly and splendidly ruins (he does not nourish) his own family certainly does have a great need. One who determines to leave behind to his heirs a huge wealth does have a great need. Whoever needs much will likewise use many lawful and sinful means for this endeavor so that he may obtain what he has planned. These things are highlighted, and it will not seem so difficult, not only to abandon this detestable usury, but also to succor the needs of the brethren by whatever means.

## Concerning the Usury of Those Who Give Their Own Money for Usury either to Merchants or to Princes

Up to this point, we have examined that kind of usury by which a poor man is obligated to the rather wealthy and the resources of the weak and destitute are devoured. After that, we spoke about that kind of loan to which Christ orders us in order to succor the needs of the brethren. Now I must speak about those who, using their own money that has been acquired by inheritance or from some other source, give it to the wealthy, to businessmen, or to princes, by that law, so that they may receive something in the place of usury either for a monthly or annual payment for a space of time, meanwhile keeping the whole share, so that whenever they wish they can call it back. Here this question arises: What is the sin in this kind of usury? They say that it is not burdensome, either for the person who gives or receives usury, and indeed it beautifully considers the advantages of both parties. Whoever gives usury uses the share of that well, and he gains so much from that share that he could give without any loss. On the other hand, whoever receives usury from his own money gathers certain fruit each year without any detriment to his share, and, for this reason, it can be preserved intact for the use of his heirs. Therefore, because there is no disadvantage here, how is it a sin against charity? If there is no sin, how can it be said about this kind of usury that it is unlawful?

I respond: Indeed it must be entirely admitted that this kind of usury is not as much of a sin as that by which usury is received from the weak, something that is not only condemned as inhuman by the laws of Christ, but also by the laws of nature. It is plainly inhuman to pursue a profit from the sweat and calamities of the poor. Therefore, that type of usury of which we are now about to speak differs the most from the previous type, which absolutely cannot be tolerated. Meanwhile, to be sure, it must not be thought that there is nothing in this usury of wealth that can be reprehended. In fact, the justice of a Christian man does not rest with the result that he does not burden anyone in any business. It must be considered what the circumstances of this usury are on account of which it is done, so that it cannot be commended. First, what I think is fitting is that both agree, inasmuch as the one who gives and the one who receives usury have each provided for his own advantage. As a matter of fact, no one contracts his own money to a wealthy businessman on account of brotherly charity, but rather in order that he may receive a monthly or annual benefit from it. Likewise, that businessman is not eager to give usury, because if he could delay it to his own advantage, he would. For as that proverb says, "the love of money grows as the money itself grows." Yet, he gives usury without delay in order to avoid having to restore the whole share and to avoid incurring a letter of bad faith. There are notorious, conspicuous examples of this business. When the root of this kind of usury is the pursuit of one's own advantage, I do not see how it could be suitable and without any fault for Christians, to whom the pursuit of their own advantage ought to be most foreign. "Let no one seek those things which are his own," says the apostle, "but those things which are for another" [1 Cor. 10:24]. Indeed that is rather unusual, however much it may be endured among the Gentiles who are eager for their own advantage to the detriment of others. Yet, in itself, even without another person's loss, desiring one's own advantage ought to be foreign to Christians, just as it should be strange for Christians to be luxurious or at leisure, even though it can be done without others' disadvantage and loss. Therefore, just as they sin who are luxuriating in the houses of princes, magnates, and the wealthy, although they may perceive no loss, likewise a Christian errs if he is greedy for his own advantage, even if his intent is such that he seeks his own advantage not from the scarcity of the poor but from the opulence of the wealthy.

Furthermore, we must investigate whether or not someone who receives usury is a slave to his own unbelief. For instance, it is unsatisfactory for a Christian person to act in such a way with his neighbor as if he does not have what his neighbor may seek, but rather he must consider what faith toward God is and how what he does is either consistent or inconsistent with sincere faith. In order that the experience of this matter may be grasped, let him consider with respect to himself (whoever accepts usury), that it is better to keep back for himself his own money and to recoil from the gain of usury. If someone lacks faith, immediately these thoughts arise: "If I must not live by usury, but from that share, it would not suffice for the necessary costs throughout my whole life. Next, what is left after my death for my children and posterity?" From there he proceeds to: "What will I live upon, if I should consume it all?" Those thoughts are not from faith but from a lack of faith, and souls that are given in this way to usury argue that they think to themselves that they would not have the resources to live if they should relinquish usury. It is objected: "Do not test the Lord" [Deut. 6:6; Matt. 4:7; Luke 4:12]—as if testing the Lord is to depend upon his providence with a firm faith according to the word of God and to refuse to live that kind of life in which necessities are obtained by idleness through the pursuit of usury. If to be unwilling to live off of usury is to test the Lord, I ask how so many pious people among the Old and New Testament fathers, prophets, apostles, and others are defended who underwent penury rather than embrace the gain of usury? Therefore, does Christ teach his own to test the Lord when he commands that they are not to amass for themselves treasure vaults and that they are to give a loan hoping for nothing from it? To test the Lord is to have confidence in the Lord where there is no promise from the Lord, and to neglect the reasons for living and God's prescriptions for acting, and instead to use other means. Moreover, nowhere do I find that the Lord has promised that he wishes us to preserve and nourish ourselves by usury in leisure and luxury. Therefore, rather, what it is to test the Lord is to live in leisure, to dedicate one's children also to leisure, and meanwhile to hope that the money that is annually received by usury will be able to provide perpetually so that one may be a slave not only to necessary enjoyments, but also to luxuries and delicacies.

Therefore, also, that objection of theirs is frivolous, when, as they cloak their own usury, they say, "Ich muß mein gelt vuagen" ("I must risk my money"). That is to say, "I commit my money for the sake of usury to a foreign trust; I contract it out with discrimination. It can happen that a merchant who uses my money for his own business, either through a misfortune or by his own negligence, may become poor, and thus my whole share may go to waste. Therefore, by no means is this truly iniquity because I receive the usury from that investment while fortune smiles." Thus, a usurer fluctuates unsure and devotes his own affairs to risks, which is foreign to those who labor with faith toward God, which is suitable for an honest man. Gamblers also subject their own money to an uncertain risk, yet for this reason no sane person approves of a zeal for gambling in a Christian person. In this way, although they confess that they are unwilling to be the kind who test God not only in deed but also in words because they devote their money to uncertain events and risks when they contract out their money for the sake of usury, in such a way they do test God.

Third, it must also be considered how a wealthy man, a business man, or a prince, from whom you take usury, conducts himself. You think it is enough to excuse usury that insofar as the recipient of the loan is not poor, giving your own things for usury is not troublesome. Indeed, if you will rightly think it over, you will understand that still other things must be observed. For instance, if that wealthy man, business man, or prince applies force in this matter so that he abuses your money, either for the pursuit of wealth or a contemptible thing and luxury, or for the exercise of tyranny, or for some bellicose business, even sometimes for the devastation and oppression of a country or region, I beseech you, how could you boast that the usury you accept is not culpable when for the sake of usury you are a slave to another's sins while you make your money subject to the wantonness of such a person? Do you not think that you take part in that use for which you contract your money, but merely in how it goes with your profit? Should the luxuries of our age, the feasts that are more than those of the Gentiles, such shameful haste of many thousands, so many commotions and casualties of wars, the plundering of subordinates—should these daily increase all for the sake of usury? What now of that money that is contracted out by usury? If you are a Christian, how could you have no account for these things? It is just as if there is a certain conspiracy made between those who give and those who accept usury. They discuss among themselves the borrowed aid in which it may serve either their very own advantages or dispositions, and thus among themselves they are united for sinning. It is weighty if someone sins individually and privately. How much more weighty ought it seem if someone expends his own aid in such a way for his neighbor for the sake of his own advantage so that he may furnish the kindling for wickedness?

Fourth, it also ought to be considered how this kind of usury may impede the works of charity. A usurer tries to contract his own money, which is idle and not compelled by any present necessity for domestic uses, for some use so that it may not remain idle and fruitless, but that he may raise something profitable from it. Therefore, he contracts it out for usury, and for this reason he thinks this is the best way to look out for his own business. Possessed of this spirit, I entreat you, when will he help neighbors who have become poor and destitute all around him? What he raises from usury, he partly assigns for necessary uses and partly for profit, to increase the share more each year by which it could grow. When do you think he will give to the destitute? When will he give a loan to a poor man seeking one freely and without usury? When does he nourish himself and his own from it? I do not think he does. "How can I give to others," he asks, "out of that which I personally need?" Paul says, "so that from your abundance, one may supply the lack of others" [2 Cor. 8:14]. In this case, there is no abundance. "That which I have is necessary—all of it. It must be arranged that I should adorn this standing that I have received from my ancestors. I should have the reckoning of my name and honor. I will bring up a wife and children not basely and meagerly but liberally, as is proper." This need is not a definite, moderate, and usual amount, but an exceedingly great and splendid amount of money. Will he give out of that which he plans for usury? By no means! He does not think these things strike at holy things. What therefore remains standing except that in such a person the works of charity are suppressed by the pursuit of amassing money—particularly if that usury is believed to be unlawful, so that the love of money (φιλαργυρία) has seized his breast? He is stung by no sense of sin, but thinks that in a lawful thing there is no danger. Hence, we hear these expressions when something is sought as a loan from such persons: "I would give," they say, "a loan if the money were available, but at present there is no money, therefore I give nothing. I am looking out for my own good." Thus, they excuse their neglect of the work of charity. However, why is there no money at hand? For the reason, of course, that part of it is for domestic and daily expenses and the other part has been assigned to the enriching and accumulating of the share. Hence, we seem to have come to the point that those who have been devoted to this manner of usury do not readily render a payment due to either laborers, or tailors, or shoemakers, but they allow great sums to grow over several years so that they may not be compelled to cut anything whatsoever from the money for either usury or domestic goods. Meanwhile, however, they diminish the domestic goods of the workers to whom they owe payment. In this matter, what could be thought more iniquitous?

If those things that I have examined up to this point are weighed, it is evident how this particular kind of usury is a kindling for our own advantage and serves unbelief and a lack of faith. Abuse attends to money that has been contracted out for usury, and just as works of charity are scuttled by the pursuit of collecting money, I believe that it is abundantly clear that not even that kind of usury that is practiced among the rather opulent, as if it is lawful, can be practiced by those who are cognizant of what is required by professors of the Christian faith, whose fraternal countersigns are charity and a contempt for worldly resources, so that those who lack these countersigns cannot be counted as Christians.

## Concerning Usury for Widows and Orphans

Whoever are protectors of either widows or orphans produce this question in this place: Whether it is lawful for them to contract out, not their own money, but the money of widows and orphans from the inheritance left by their ancestors, and to hand over their money to uses that return some interest each year without any of loss to the widows and orphans. "The money is not ours," they say, "but entrusted to us for safekeeping. What we do, we do not for ourselves but for the advantage of widows and orphans. Let us ask why we are culpable in this as if we received usury for ourselves. For we ask not for ourselves, but for others—see it is all right for widows and for orphans, it is for their advantage—and, in such a manner, we fulfill a work of charity. We also satisfy our trust by which we are bound to them."

I respond: It is not unknown to me what was the custom of our ancestors before the plague of usury profaned the church so that what previously was permitted to no one should now be permitted for widows and orphans. All usury was notorious, not just for widows and orphans. Finally, all the valves for this evil have been opened and the gain of usury has been permitted to everyone. Indeed, how well-practiced it is among widows and orphans to follow the corruption of our times shows more clearly than the sun. A more harmful evil could not be introduced into the Christian church, by which it begins to be troublesome in the affairs of widows and orphans in wretched ways. As a matter of fact, while the domestic fortunes are squandered in the fire by usury, I ask what is left behind for the widows and orphans after the death of the head of the family since he had contracted out for usury. Can it be that it would be a better decision for the widows and orphans if the license for usury has no place among Christians? Now, since the gain of usury is admitted under the pretext of being for widows and orphans, it is not so great a thing for those of our time to accept usury as suitable, however much evil and trouble arose from that concession to our ancestors.

Next, in fact, that concession to our ancestors sufficiently proves that usury should not be permitted for widows and orphans because of the mere reason that it was lawful. Besides, to what extent did it restrain the permitting and indulging of it when it was lawful and irreprehensible? It was thought that it could be permitted to widows and orphans in this way although it was illicit for everyone else, especially because charity—that mother of all beneficence—began not only to grow cold and also sterile, but began to die off. If the apostolic prescription concerning widows in 1 Timothy 5[:3–16] is preserved, by all means it would look out for widows much better and in a more Christian manner than through the grant of illicit usury. If the widow is younger, she should work at something honest and either be a servant born from humbler birth or she should be subservient to her ancestors until an occasion is pleasantly given by the Lord to marry. If she is more advanced in age, she should live from her own resources simply, as long as her resources last. Once those have been consumed, she should be supported either by her relatives or, if that cannot be done, by the provision of the church in the custom of the apostolic church. At the beginning of the forming of the church of the faithful the resources of the church were amassed by contribution. How were they dispensed?

They were divided exactly as anyone had need; they were not contracted out to usurers for revenue. That simplicity was suitable for the Christian faith, and it was commending that charity with whose authority the disciples of Christ are acquainted. Now, it is declared daily by exceedingly many examples how much more in this age of usury the necessity of widows and orphans must be looked after by this kind of faith.

Yet, if the remaining chaos of usury and illicit contracts are to be destroyed from a community in which the usury that looks to the necessities of widows, orphans, and those in poorhouses is so easily tolerated, it will be either by the authority of the word of God among those who wish to appear to fear God, or by the power of the magistrates. (It should not be a worry in the next imperial elections, if in fact, as it is pretended, a reformation of the Christian church is sought!) Therefore, it must be desired from this spirit: that if all usury in the whole world cannot be eliminated from the church of Christ, at least let those kinds be removed in which the substance of the weak are plundered in such miserable ways contrary to Christian charity. Nay more, let the lenders be entirely consumed in such a way that they can endure the interest-bearing losses out of a disposition of true love, according to the heart of Christ our Savior, either by bountifully giving or by giving a loan—a hand stretching out to the destitute that is responsible not to plunder but to assist.

Against this kind of usury the experts in canon law (*Canonistae*) assigned to usurers appropriate penalties more than simply the divine reproach. First, usurers are defamed by the disrepute of the law—even the civil law, not to speak of the canonical law. Next, they ought not to be admitted to the ecclesiastical communion. Third, they ought to be excluded from ecclesiastical burial. Fourth, their wills are not to be ratified by any law, with several other just kinds of censures. Indeed, those censures remained on the books without effect, and meanwhile honors of all kinds followed the usurers, together with their unlawful wealth, into the church. Moreover, such great impudence prevailed with impunity so that the majority of magistrates, princes, as well as the rest of the magnates, and also the Jews, made a sum for their own dominions not through simple usury but by what the usurers call cultivating usury. They do not only make a sum, but they also contract out for temples, and by certain exactions contract with the borrowers something that they ought to pay out each year on account of the grant of usury. Finally, also most unjustly they compel their own subordinates in such a way that by paying such usury they are guilty. Here, those pontifical censures remain quiet, turning a blind eye to the ravens and tearing apart the doves.

At last we assign an end to these considerations upon usury. As I mentioned in the beginning, it can plainly be esteemed folly to be occupied in several things in a kind of business that is like gout that does not receive the attention of any doctor's hand. This evil has grown up continuously to such a degree that after the admonition of many good men has been made, it is incurable. For it corrupts those highest heads who had the authority to oppose these kinds of corruptions and to direct and guide their subjected members into the pursuit of true righteousness. The saying of Christ is: "If the salt should lose its saltiness, how will it be made salty again?" [Matt. 5:13; Mark 9:50; Luke 14:34]. Likewise: "You are the light of the world. If the light which is in you should become dark, how great will the darkness of the body be?" [Luke 11:36]. What remains is to await the hand of the Lord who soon will destroy every kind of corruption from his church. In the end, he will come, and he will free his own. Amen and Amen.

# About the Contributors

**Jordan J. Ballor** (Dr. theol., University of Zurich) is a research fellow at the Acton Institute for the Study of Religion & Liberty and serves as executive editor of the *Journal of Markets & Morality*. He is also the author of *Covenant, Causality, and Law: A Study in the Theology of Wolfgang Musculus* (Vandenhoeck & Ruprecht, 2012) and *Ecumenical Babel: Confusing Economic Ideology and the Church's Social Witness* (Christian's Library Press, 2010).

**Stephen J. Grabill** (PhD, Calvin Theological Seminary) serves as senior research scholar in theology and director of programs at the Acton Institute for the Study of Religion & Liberty. He is editor emeritus of the *Journal of Markets & Morality*, as well as author of *Rediscovering the Natural Law in Reformed Theological Ethics* (Eerdmans, 2006) and editor of *Sourcebook in Late-Scholastic Monetary Theory* (Lexington, 2007).

**Todd M. Rester** (PhD cand., Calvin Theological Seminary) is director of the Junius Institute for Digital Reformation Research at Calvin Theological Seminary and translator of numerous works, including William Ames, *A Sketch of the Christian's Catechism*, and Petrus van Mastricht, *Theologia theoretico-practica.*

Christian's LIBRARY PRESS

Founded in 1979 by Gerard Berghoef and Lester DeKoster, **Christian's Library Press** has been committed to publishing influential texts on church leadership, the vocation of work, and stewardship for more than thirty years. During that time Berghoef and DeKoster wrote significant works including *The Deacons Handbook*, *The Elders Handbook*, and *God's Yardstick*, which still are in demand today. After the passing of Lester DeKoster in 2009, the imprint is now administered by the Acton Institute for the Study of Religion & Liberty. For more information about Christian's Library Press, visit www.clpress.com.

## ACTON INSTITUTE

With its commitment to pursue a society that is free and virtuous, the **Acton Institute for the Study of Religion & Liberty** is a leading voice in the international environmental and social policy debate. With offices in Grand Rapids, Michigan, and Rome, Italy, as well as affiliates in four other nations around the world, the Acton Institute is uniquely positioned to comment on the sound economic and moral foundations necessary to sustain humane environmental and social policies. The Acton Institute is a nonprofit, ecumenical think tank working internationally to "promote a free and virtuous society characterized by individual liberty and sustained by religious principles." For more on the Acton Institute, please visit www.acton.org.

## Sources in Early Modern Economics, Ethics, and Law

*Jordan J. Ballor and Stephen J. Grabill, General Editors*

### Books in This Series

*A Treatise on the Alteration of Money*
**Juan de Mariana**
Translated by Patrick T. Brannan • Annotations by Stephen J. Grabill
Introduction by Alejandro A. Chafuen

*On the Law in General*
**Girolamo Zanchi**
Translated by Jeffrey J. Veenstra • Introduction by Stephen J. Grabill

*On Law and Power*
**Johannes Althusius**
Translated by Jeffrey J. Veenstra • Introductions by Stephen J. Grabill and John Witte Jr.

*On Exchange and Usury*
**Thomas Cajetan**
Translated by Patrick T. Brannan • Introduction by Raymond de Roover

*On Righteousness, Oaths, and Usury*
**Wolfgang Musculus**
Translated by Todd M. Rester • Introduction by Jordan J. Ballor

*On Exchange*
**Martín de Azpilcueta**
Translated by Jeannine Emery • Introduction by Rodrigo Muñoz

*A Treatise on Money*
**Luis de Molina**
Translated by Jeannine Emery • Introduction by Rudolf Schuessler

*The Mosaic Polity*
**Franciscus Junius**
Translated by Todd M. Rester • Edited by Andrew M. McGinnis

*Of the Law of Nature*
**Matthew Hale**
Edited by David S. Sytsma

*On Sale, Securities, and Insurance*
**Leonardus Lessius**
Translated by Wim Decock and Nicholas De Sutter • Introduction by Wim Decock

Made in the USA
Monee, IL
13 September 2026

62981867R00095